MONTENEGRO: THE DIVIDED LAND by Thomas Fleming

16

MONTENEGRO
THE DIVIDED LAND

by Thomas Fleming

Chronicles Press
Rockford, Illinois

ISBN 0-9619364-9-5

Contents

PREFACE

Although the decision to write the history of Montenegro was made all too recently, the genesis of this book goes back two years, to a glorious December afternoon in Grbalj. My friends and I had spent the morning at an Orthodox liturgy conducted on the grounds of a ruined church, which His Eminence the Metropolitan Amfilohije hoped to restore (as he has done with so many Montenegrin churches). We had come the day before from Belgrade, which was digging out from a massive blizzard, but here we were, wearing nothing heavier than tweed jackets and standing out in the bright sunlight that warmed the Adriatic coast. As the Metropolitan finished his homily, a cheer went up and an explosion knocked me off my feet. Dusting myself off and looking around for terrorists, I was hit again by what seemed to be a great cannonade. No, it was not NATO forces launching rockets at an Orthodox liturgy, only Montenegrins lighting sticks of dynamite to celebrate the feast Sveti Sava, much as lesser people light firecrackers on New Year's Eve.

We spent the afternoon at a private house in Grbalj, eating an unending feast that Penelope might have prepared to welcome home her wandering husband. When we had eaten and drunk our fill, a bard in traditional costume entered the room, and after playing an elaborate prelude on his one-stringed *gusle*, an instrument that sounds like nothing so much as a bagpipe, the guslar launched into a recital of the exploits of some brave Montenegrin hero, but whether he was getting married, fighting Turks, or merely raiding cattle, I could not tell.

At the end of the guslar's performance, the Metropolitan joked that his father had been a guslar, and that, as a child sitting in his father's lap, he too had learned the art. Nonsense, his people said affectionately, his Eminence was making a joke. Calling for the *gusle*, he stuck up a brilliant and ornate prelude to an ancient tale.

During the performance, the entire company was rapt, and one of our hosts—a tall, black-haired man in a leather jacket—walked to the open window and contemplated the blue Adriatic that stretched out before him. With an almost beatific look, he reached into his jacket—for a cigarette I thought—and, pulling out a .45 automatic, emptied the clip, firing at the point where the blue sea meets the blue sky. I leaned over and said to one of my friends, "We might have stepped into a lost book of the *Odyssey*." This was not the land of the Lotus-eaters who took drugs to forget everything, but of the hajduks and guslars who forget nothing. If I had another lifetime, I thought to myself, I might spend it improving my Serbian and learning to tell the story of Montenegro as the Metropolitan tells it, going legend by legend and from one ruin to another.

Alas, as things turned out, I would have not another lifetime but only a few months in which to complete a history that will explain to the world what both Serbia and Montenegro have to lose if they proceed with their divorce. This book would not have been possible without the active assistance and support of many people: my research assistant Ljiljana, who helped with translation of texts; E. Christian Kopff, who gave valuable help on ancient historians; the many friends in or from the Balkans who provided help and encouragement in this project; and my wife and children who endured the several months in which the author turned into a hibernating bear that emerged from his computer-lit cave only to growl at the world and talk endlessly about the crime of Staniša Crnojević or the heroic exploits of the Piperi and the Grbljani.

ILLYRIA

"And what should I do in Illyria?"
—Shakespeare, *Twelfth Night*

The harsh and beautiful land of Montenegro is an enigma and not merely to outsiders. The Montenegrins themselves have never quite made up their minds if their country is a geographical territory, a nation-state, or an important part of a greater Serbia. With a land mass (5,333 square miles) roughly that of Northern Ireland or the state of Connecticut and a population (about 600,000) roughly the same as Dublin's, Montenegro, with its variety of landscape and cultures and the richness of its historical traditions, can seem as large as France and Italy and far greater than nations many times its size.[1]

Confusion over the Montenegrin identity begins with the name "Montenegro" itself. Why should a Slavic country be known by what looks like a Spanish name? *Montenegro* is, in fact, a Venetian dialect form of the standard Italian *Monte Nero*, which is a translation of *Crna Gora* or "black mountain," a name that Serbs were applying, by the 15th century, to the mountains that rise up from the Montenegrin coast. Like other Serbs, Montenegrins belong, for the most part, to the Orthodox Church, and their language is one of the Western Serbian dialects, close to what is spoken in Hercegovina and on the Croatian littoral. Despite the arguments advanced by various ethnic groups staking historical claims over the region, there are no "pure" races in the Balkans. During the past three millennia the lands of Montenegro (like those of Albania, Croatia, and Serbia) have been overrun by Illyrians, Dalmatians, Celts, Greeks, Macedonians, Romans, Goths, Slavs, Venetians, Turks, and Austrians—all of whom have left genetic and cultural footprints among the people. The old proverb about Balkan land disputes remains true today: Whatever nation holds the most ancient claim to a land will not be the nation in present possession.

The present-day Yugoslav republic of Montenegro is an eagle's nest hewn from the rough karst of the Dinaric Alps, sloping in the West toward a brief coastline along the Adriatic that stretches from Albania in the south to the region of Konavle, a coastal strip below Dubrovnik (in today's Croatia) in the north. This "shower of granite thrown from heaven" is bordered on the East by Serbia and on the North by Bosnia-Hercegovina. This geography is a primary reality in Montenegrin history, since the mountain regions have typically looked eastward, while the coastal areas have typically been drawn into a Western (often Italian) orbit. Metternich expressed his contempt for Italian nationalism by describing Italy as a geographical expression. That is more than he could have said of Montenegro, which has been more often divided than united by its geography.

The first traces of human settlement in the region date from the Paleolithic period. Artifacts—mostly tools, hunting weapons, jewelry, and religious paraphernalia—have been found in several parts of Montenegro, *e.g.*, in the Crvena Stijena (Red Rock) cave above Lake Bileća, and a rich set of finds illustrates the continuity of settlement throughout the Mesolithic and Neolithic periods. The earlier settlements, down to the Iron Age, give evidence of a connected culture region extending from Southwestern Serbia through Montenegro to Albania, but during the late Iron Age (fourth to first centuries B.C.), differences emerge between the less developed highland areas and the coastal strip, which came under Greek and Roman influences.[2]

Montenegro, perhaps because of its location, has had a strong attraction for the most violent and adventurous peoples. Of all the Greeks that went in search of colonies, trade, and plunder, none were bolder or more fiercely independent than the people of Phocaea, the northernmost of the Ionian cities on Asia Minor. Herodotus says they were the first Greeks to undertake long voyages, and Phocaean merchants strung out a series of trading posts across the Mediterranean, founding Masillia (Marseilles) on the way to Spain. In 540, hopelessly outnumbered by the Persian army, the Phocaeans asked for a truce of one day to consider the surrender terms. Within 24 hours, they managed to sail away with their wives and children to Chios. Forced to move, they stopped back in Phocaea before setting out for Corsica and put the entire Persian garrison to the sword. Half the Phocaeans chose to remain behind in their native city, but these timid souls were to distinguish themselves in the Ionian Revolt against Persia. In Corsica, they took up the lucrative career of piracy, but driven from Corsica by the Etruscans and Carthaginians, they settled in southern Italy, where they founded Elea, a city that was to become famous for philosophy.[3]

These Phocaean Greeks were exploring the Adriatic coast by the sixth century B.C., and if they left any of their red blood behind, it has not been watered down by the other progenitors of the Montenegrin people. Greek explorers could not have provided very accurate information on Dalmatia: Until even the fourth century, it was widely believed that the Adriatic and Black Seas almost touched each other. In the late sixth century Hecataeus of Miletus provided a geographical and ethnic sketch of the area, but it is not until 330 that we have a surviving written document—the *Periplous* ("circumnavigation") of a writer who tried to pass himself as the old Seadog Skylax. He and later writers list the tribes who live along the coast. The Liburnians were probably the first people known to history, who settled the Adriatic coast of Dalmatia, Montenegro, and Albania—all the way to Corfu, from which (according to tradition) they were expelled by Corinth in the eighth century.[4] The Illyrians were the next people to dominate the Adriatic coast, and one Illyrian tribe, the Enchelei were said to have lived around Kotor Bay (Boka Kotorska).[5]

The interior of Montenegro (and of Illyria as a whole) presents a different picture. Though comparatively little is known of these regions until Roman times, they had been settled by Illyrian and Venetic tribes as well as by Pannonians. The uplands of northeastern Dalmatia and much of Serbia had also been invaded by the Celts, who may have extended their influence into parts of Montenegro, though no evidence of Celtic settlements has been found there. Celtic remains have been found in the valleys of the Drina and the Morava rivers, but Belgrade itself was also a Celtic settlement. Celtic influence on the Serbs is largely a matter of speculation, though Slavs and Celts lived in proximity in northern Europe before the Slavic migrations to the Balkans, and Serbs of the mountainous regions continue to display many physical and cultural traits associated with the Celtic type: tall men, more brave than disciplined, pasturing herds and flocks in the woods and hillsides rather than growing grain, more fond of singing songs and telling stories than founding institutions.

The Illyrians, who gave their name to the region, were tough warriors who spoke an Indo-European language (as did the Greeks, Romans, Celts, and Slavs who entered the region). They had lived in Kosovo before spreading southward to confront the Macedonians. By the 390's, Bardylis, an Illyrian chief "who probably ruled the area around Lake Ochrid," was raiding and plundering northern Macedonia and even succeeded in driving Amyntas III, the father of Philip II, temporarily from the throne.[6] Athough Amyntas tried to buy off Bardylis by paying tribute, the Illyrians continued to plague Macedonia until Philip (382-36 B.C.) decisively defeated the Illyrians at Lake Lychnitis in 358 and subjugated all of Illyria—with the significant exception of the coastline.[7] In the early third century, Pyrrhus of Epirus (319-272) annexed southern Illyria to his extensive dominions.

After previously establishing colonies at Epidmanus (seventh century) and Apollonia (sixth century), the Greeks began to develop trading contacts in Dalmatia, and, in the fourth century, they were planting colonies along the Adriatic Coast from Korčula (Melaina Kerkyra) in Croatia to Lissus (Lješ) in Albania, including a settlement at Bothoe (the modern sea resort of Budva), which was said to have been founded by Phoenician Cadmus after his expulsion from Boeotia. These Greek colonies were subjugated, early in the third century B.C., by the Illyrian kingdom established by the Ardiaei clan, which increased its strength later in the century under Pleuratas I (d. 260) and his son Agron. This kingdom was headquartered around Lake Scutari (lying on the border between modern Albania and Montenegro), and the Illyrians, who learned to exploit the advantages of their location, made themselves famous for piracy, sailing in small galleys (*lembi*) that carried only a single bank of oars but provided room for 50 fighting men.

The political pattern of the Balkans was established early, in the relations between Illyrians and Macedonians (and later the Romans). So long as the Macedonian kingdom was strong, it could subjugate most of Illyria and contain the periodic outbreaks of piracy, but as soon as Macedonian power grew slack, an ambitious Illyrian ruler was waiting to take advantage of the opportunity. Phillip II and his son, Alexander the Great, were able to subdue most of Illyria, apart from the troublesome coastal region, but the weakness of later Macedonian rulers allowed the Illyrians to rebuild their strength, and, in the late third century, the Illyrian King Agron sent ships to support Macedonia against the Aetolian League in Greece. Agron controlled territories from northern Dalmatia all the way to southern Albania across from the heel of Italy, and his ships caused considerable annoyance to Greek merchants.

Under Agron's widow and successor, Teuta (who may have given her name to Tivat), Illyrian pirates attacked Sicily and the Greek colonies of the Italian coast. Teuta was actually ruling as regent for Agron's son born to another wife, Triteuta. She not only raided shipping but kidnapped and held for ransom some Italian merchants—which brought her to the notice of the rising power in Italy. When Rome sent ambassadors to negotiate, Teuta made the mistake of treating their peremptory demands with contempt. Whether we think Teuta was recklessly provoking Rome or simply responding to Roman arrogance, may depend on our point of view. Like Elizabeth I of England, she profited from piracy, and, like Elizabeth, she was determined to resist a domineering power committed to putting down this profitable activity.[8]

After Demetrius of Pharos betrayed Corfu to the Romans (and married Triteuta), Teuta was forced to submit in 228 and sent into seclusion within Illyria. Rome laid down the significant condition that no more than two Illyrian ships could sail at one time south of Lissus. This was meant to secure Greek and Italian shipping on the Ionian sea. As a result of her victory of the Illyrians, The Romans established "friendship" with Corcyra, Apollonia, and Epidamnus (Dyracchium), making themselves *de facto* the masters of the Adriatic. But Illyria was not completely subdued until the three Illyrian Wars (in 229-28, 219, and 107-8) that the Romans waged as an interlude and postscript to their greater struggles with Carthage.

The Adriatic coast has always been a center of piracy and smuggling, often organized by the local rulers. The Illyrians had not learned that it is dangerous to attract the attention of a rising imperial state that seeks to impose law and order. Pleuratas II appears to have read the writing on the wall, and, throughout his reign, Illyria passively supported Rome.[9] However, his successor Genthius (180-68) resumed his nation's profession of piracy and tried to play Rome and Macedon, who were in a bidding war for his support, off against each other. Finally, Genthius (who is described by pro-Roman historians as an intemperate drinker and prone to violence) made the fatal decision to support King Perseus of Macedon against Rome. In 168, a Roman praetor (Lucius Anicius Gallus) led his army against Scodra (later Scutari, known to the Serbs as Skadar), stormed the city, and captured the unfortunate king.[10] The Romans drove the Ardiaei into the interior, where they passed from history. Their place was taken by another native tribe, the Delmatae, who moved into the power vacuum that had opened up along the Adriatic coast.

Balkan political leaders are sometimes considered unreliable and tricky by the great empires that demand unswerving loyalty from the peoples over whom they are attempting to exercise hegemony. Illyrian and Delmatic rulers were no exception in looking after their own interests: They no sooner made an alliance with Rome or Macedon than they proceeded to violate it. Rome eventually turned the entire area into a Roman province, employing the classic Roman tactic of *divide et impera*, supporting an allied Greek community (Issa, modern Vis) against the Delmatae, who lived along the central and northern Adriatic coastline. Roman troops decisively defeated the Delmatae in 155, though coastal towns like Olcinium (Ulcinj) continued to be accused of harboring pirates.[11]

Small countries that engage in power politics with great empires are like the proverbial clay pots floating in the company of iron pans. The inevitable result is a smash-up, even when the imperial state has no important interests at stake. The Romans do not appear to have formed a uniform strategy for taking over the Illyria. They had been drawn in, incident by incident, in response to what they regarded as provocation, but once their interest was aroused, the Romans were virtually unstoppable. Illyria's final chapter was written by Julius Caesar, who went there twice, both to learn about the country and to investigate reports of piracy. Illyricum had been allotted to Caesar (along with Cisalpine Gaul) for his proconsulate, and he regularly wintered in Aquileia, just across the Adriatic.[12] Julius decided he had to defend his defenseless allies—the same pretext he used for conquering Gaul.

The Delmatae and their allies supported Pompey against Caesar, and during the difficult times of the civil wars of the late first century B.C., neither of Caesar's would-be heirs, Mark Antony and Octavian, was able to impose the Pax Romana on Illyria. In their meeting at Brundisium in 40 B.C., before the fate of the world was decided, the rivals had agreed to divide the empire into two parts.[13] Significantly, the dividing line ran through Scodra, at the foot of the mountains of Montenegro. The coastal areas belonged to Europe—and Octavian. The lands east of the mountains went to Antony, the ruler of Egypt and Asia.

Octavian campaigned against the Iapudes and Pannonians in 35 and then against the Delmatae in 34-33. He was so confident of the results that Illyricum was granted the status of a senatorial province (implying it was pacified) between 27 and 11 B.C.[14] Octavian (now titled Augustus) was disabused by the Pannonian War (6-9 A.D.). The three-year long uprising was led by Bato, chief of the Daesitiates (a Pannonian tribe living in the region of today's Sarajevo), and (as the emperor boasts) pushed the Roman frontier up to the Danube. It was not an easy campaign, but (as Suetonius described it) "the most serious of foreign wars since the Punic,"[15] requiring the talents of the emperor's two most talented heirs,

Tiberius and Germanicus. After surrendering to the Romans, Bato defended his conduct, charging Augustus with sending "as guardians of your flocks not shepherds or dogs but wolves." Bato, who had clearly won the respect of his opponents, was granted an honorable retirement in Ravenna[16], and Illyricum was divided into two provinces, Dalmatia and Pannonia. Rome consolidated its Balkan possessions in the early second century, when the Emperor Trajan moved into Dacia and conquered the warlike tribes of what is now Rumania.

The coastal regions enjoyed peace and prosperity, but the hinterlands of Montenegro and Hercegovina were sparsely settled. The city of Doclea,[17] near modern Podgorica, was the most important settlement away from the coast. Until Doclea became a Roman *municipium*, the area was ruled by tribal chieftains who continued to exercise considerable authority in so remote a place. The contrast between the rich material remains of the coastal settlements and the scanty evidence in the interior give a strong indication that the process of Romanization was not nearly so effective in the hinterlands as along the littoral.[18]

The region of Illyria not only flourished under Roman rule but also produced some of the most effective soldiers and emperors who shored up the crumbling empire in the fourth and fifth centuries A.D. (The officers responsible for guarding the Danube frontier were known as *Illyriciani*.) The most important of them, Diocletian, probably took his name, ultimately, from the town of Doclea in Montenegro. Diocletian, despite his military profession, was not an especially blood-thirsty ruler, but his obsession with preserving the unity of the empire led him to acquiesce in his colleague's desire to eliminate the problem of Christianity by torturing and killing as many of the Christians as they could lay their hands on. In Montenegro, he has entered into legend both as a symbol of power and as the evil Car Dukljanin who enflamed animosities and persecuted the faithful.

Diocletian was a good though not brilliant soldier, but he had a genius for organization and bureaucracy (if genius is a proper term to apply to so drab a profession as imperial administration). His division of the empire into East and West, each governed by its own Augustus, was to be the basis of the ultimate split of the Empire, and although the line between Illyricum orientale (dioecesis Moesiarum) and Illyricum occidentale (dioecesis Pannoniarum) ran through the middle of the Balkans (and through Montenegro), it meant effectively that Constantinople was to become the dominant force in the region. Diocletian, exhausted from the labor of keeping the world safe for civilization, took early retirement and withdrew to his palace-complex in Split, on the Dalmatian coast, to plant cabbages (in 305).

In the civil wars of the fourth century, Illyria was somewhat off the beaten track and little mentioned by historians, though one of the most famous men of fourth century, St. Jerome, came from somewhere in Dalmatia near the Pannonian border. The death of Theodosius in 395 marked the irrevocable division of the empire, with one significant territorial adjustment. Dalmatia and Pannonia, which had belonged

Ruins of ancient Doclea

to the Western Empire, had been transferred to the East in the early fifth century, as the result of a deal between Theodosius II and Placidia, the dowager empress of the West, though the question of jurisdiction was frequently a problem and always something of a muddle—the Roman Church retained authority over the Church in Dalmatia and the Adriatic littoral. Throughout even the fifth century, the Adriatic coast was a "tranquil backwater," ignored by both East and West for the most part and quasi-independent, while the upcountry probably lapsed into rule by local chieftains.

In places like Salona (modern Split, on the Adriatic coast of Illyria), the Roman world lived on. Salona became a center of independent power under the Roman commander Marcellinus, who relied on his powerful fleet to defend his territory. The wily Roman, who grew overconfident, lost his life by interfering in Sicily. His nephew, Julius Nepos, was recognized by the Eastern Emperor Leo I as the commander of forces in Dalmatia in 473. Nepos invaded Italy and made himself the last legal Emperor of the West, sending Glycerius, his deposed rival, to Salona as bishop. Nepos was himself deposed by Odovacar, the German ruler who had decided to take Roman matters in his own hands, first by using Nepos' son, Romulus Augustulus, as his puppet, and then setting aside the puppet-emperor, without any pretense. Nepos also went to live in Salona, where he continued to be recognized by the Eastern Empire as the legitimate Emperor of the West. Nepos' assassination in 480, while relaxing the tension between Odovacar and the Eastern Empire, also turned all Illyria into a battleground between Odovacar and Constantinople.

Gothic tribes menaced both sides of the empire in the late fifth century. The Ostrogoths very nearly decided to stay in the Balkans, where they played a significant part in the internecine strife that weakened the Eastern Empire in the late fifth century. The empire, on the other hand, played its own game, adroitly setting one group of Goths against the other. When the rulers in Constantinople, in a brilliant strategic move, invited Theoderic the Ostrogoth to invade Italy and, as the representative of the legitimate empire, depose Odovacar the usurper, they rid the Balkans—and the entire Eastern Empire—of a dangerous threat. Illyria remained under at least nominal control of the Eastern Emperor until the fourth crusade, when Western crusaders captured and sacked Constantinople. The Ostrogoths did manage to seize control of much of western Illyria (though again in the name of the Eastern Emperor) and join it to their Italian kingdom, a move which may have brought some temporary stability to Dalmatia. However, by weakening the economic and political infrastructure, the Goths paved the way for the later invasions of Avars and Slavs.[19]

The Goths faced a serious problem as Arians, ruling over a people who were orthodox (in maintaining the equality of the Persons of the Trinity) and catholic (in acknowledging the authority of the universal church). However, Theoderic, the Gothic ruler of Italy and Dalmatia wanted to defuse the conflict by allowing the catholics to practice their religion. His followers (including the Arian priests) were not always so wise. Gothic power came crashing down with the advent of Justinian to the throne of Constantinople. The ambitious young ruler conceived the ambition of reestablishing the Roman Empire as it had been, defeating

Goths in Italy and (about 535) driving them out of Dalmatia. Although the Goths counterattacked with some initial success, they were unable to wrest the land from Byzantine control.

East Roman power was wellentrenched in the Balkans throughout the reign of Justinian, and the emperor established a new metropolitan see in a city he founded near his birthplace, not far from Naissus (Niš). All of Praevalitana (western Dalmatia) was subject to Justiniana Prima (the new name for ancient Tauresium, now called Caričin Grad), including the bishop of Doclea in Montenegro.[20]

Justinian failed, ultimately, to fulfill his dream of rebuilding the Roman Empire, and his successors were to face more determined enemies than the Persians and the Goths that his generals and armies defeated, while exhausting the empire's resources. His successes in the Balkans, however, were longer lasting than Belisarius' triumphs in Italy and North Africa. Down to the fourteenth century, the Byzantine Empire played a dominant role in Balkan affairs. The steady pressure from Constantinople, exerted on the battlefield and in the Church, ensured that the Serbian and Bulgarian peoples would be Orthodox, and it was only when Serbs from different regions were able to unite in opposition to Byzantium, under the leadership of the Nemanjić dynasty, that they were able to create a successful Serbian state.

Looking back at the ancient history of the Balkans, it is impossible to discern the outlines of any of the nations or identities that have taken shape in the past 15 centuries. There were no ancient peoples whose territory corresponded to modern Albania or Serbia, much less to Montenegro. To varying degrees, all of the Balkan peoples are a mixture of stocks: Illyrian, Dacian, Pannonian, Greek, and Celtic, as well as Germanic, Slavic, and Turkic. The important fact, which has never quite determined historical outcomes, is the Dinaric Alps, which separated coastal Illyria from the hinterlands. This barrier, institutionalized in the division of the Roman Empire and the Christian Church, might have been expected to produce a uniform Catholic and Western culture along the Adriatic coast. It was the pressure exerted by another fact, more powerful than geography, that kept the Montenegrin coast from becoming a province of the West (of the Franks, for example, or Venice or Croatia). That fact is the cultural and religious unity of the Serbian peoples, who—when they were united— were able to resist the ambitions of Venice, Hungary, and the Hapsburg Empire.

Notes

The best work on ancient Illyria is to be found in the work of classical scholars and ancient historians, who have naturally looked at the region primarily from the Greek and Roman point of view.

1. Stanojević, "Crna Gora" distinguishes four regions: 1) rocky mountains; 2) limestone highlands, less barren; 3) forested region which, with the limestone highlands, covers northeastern *Crna Gora*; 4) coastal areas and lower river valleys, from Lake Scutari to Adriatic, where, because of better climate, there are different soils.

2. Marković & Vujičić, pp. 15-31.3. Herodotus I. 163-68.

4. Apollonius Rhodius IV. 564.

5. Pseudo-Scylax c.25, cf. Wilkes, pp. 7-8.

6. Diodorus 14.92 ff., cf. Errington, pp. 29-30.

7. Errington, p. 42.

8. Appian, *Illyrica* 2-8; Walbank I, pp. 159-60.

9. Polybius 18.30, 21.9, 22.4.

10. Livy 44.30-32.

11. Wilke, p. 184.

12. Caesar BG 2.35; 5.1-21.

13. Dio 47. 21. 6; Appian BC V. 65.

14. Augustus, *Res Gestae 30.*

15. *Vit. Tib.* 16.

16. Dio 46.16.4.

17. Also Dioclea, and in Greek Doklea, and later known in Serbian as Duklja. The importance of this Roman municipium is attested to by the scope of its Roman ruins, cf. P. Mijović (1989).

18. Marković & Vujić, p. 34.

19. Fine, p. 14.

20. Justinian, Nov. XI (14 April 535; CXXXI, 3 (18 March 545), Wilkes 425.

THE RISE OF ZETA

The Romans had built their empire well out of bricks and concrete, and Roman roads and bridges made it possible for messengers and armies to pass with astonishing rapidity from northern Gaul to the Balkans and the Middle East. The vast administrative system spread like an ancient tree across the European world, but as the tree aged and the sap slowly subsided from the branches into the rotting trunk, the provincials, who had by now lost the ability to defend themselves or even to take care of their own affairs, found themselves abandoned by the legions. The newcomers did not have to cut their way through a jungle or slog through trackless wastes. The barbarian hordes that swept into Gaul and Italy and Illyria traveled with ease down the old Roman roads that led straight to the opulent cities and undefended estates that were ripe for the picking.

The Mediterranean world of the sixth century was a rough-and-tumble frontier where civilized Romans, if they wished to survive and hold onto their possessions, had to learn to fight with the same savagery and determination displayed by their barbarian rivals. The Romans once again (though for the last time) proved to be up to the task. The empire of Justinian was menaced by the German invaders of Italy, Spain, and North Africa, but the Goths and Lombards were not the only peoples invading the Roman world. Bulgars, a Turkic people, were invading Moesia and Thrace, and Slavs, who had settled on the lower Danube in Wallachia (Rumania) were coming into Illyria in search of plunder—and safety from the Huns. The Slavs are thought to have come from somewhere to the northeast (perhaps the Ukraine or Belarus), and under constant attack from the peoples of the Russian steppes, they had begun to migrate westward and southward. They had come successively under the influence of Sarmatians (an Iranian people) and the Germanic Goths before being attacked and dominated by Huns and Avars.

Invading Slavs

Procopius describes two groups of invaders into the Balkans, saying they are virtually identical in language and customs: the Antes, who have been plausibly identified as the Slavic ancestors of the modern Bulgarians; and the Sclaveni, who formed the Slavic substratum of most of the peoples of the former Yugoslavia. Working in tandem, the Antes and Sclaveni were making annual raids into the Balkans during the reign of Anastasius (491-518), and the frequency and ferocity of their attacks only increased in the sixth century, when their forces were joined with (and often directed by) the Avars, a Turkic people that could storm cities as well as raid the countryside.[1] Unlike their Turkic allies, Slavs gradually turned from raiders into settlers.

Procopius, writing of Justinian's wars, describes the Slavs and Antes as a democratic people, "and all matters that bear on the interest or misfortune of the people are taken up in common."[2] Procopius adds that Slavs worship a god of lightening (probably Perun) as well as springs and nymphs. These early Slavic "nymph" are the ancestresses of the *vile* (the beautiful but dangerous fairies living in woods and mountains) who play so prominent a part in Serbian folk poetry.

Justinian was not prepared to surrender the Balkans to the invaders. In 545, Narses the Byzantine eunuch-general, leading an army of Germanic Herulians, defeated a force of Slavs in Thrace, but in a few years they were back, raiding both Thrace and Illyria. The destination was supposed to be Thessalonike, but the Slavs, deterred by the reputation of the Byzantine general Germanus, descended into Dalmatia where they settled.[3]

Justinian, with his eye on recovering Roman "global" supremacy, attempted to fortify and defend the Balkans, but within 20 years of his death in 585, the Slavs were making permanent settlements within imperial territory.[4] As these invading tribes came in, the Romanized Illyrians, Dacians, and others took to the hills, preserved some semblance of a Latin language, and were eventually called Vlachs. Their primary survivors today are the Rumanians. Albanians, who derive from a similar ethnic background, represent a broad linguistic mix of modern Romance and Slavic elements with ancient Dacian and Illyrian.

There were also pockets of Romano-Illyrian communities along the coast, and although they were gradually merged with the Slavic invaders, some cultural and ethnic ambiguity is still easily detectable in Dalmatia and on the Montenegrin littoral, where distinctions, for example, between

Serbs and Croats have often been more blurred than distinct. As late as 1890 Simo Matavulj, in describing the friendly relations between Catholics and Orthodox in Boka Kotorska, declared that the Catholics still considered themselves Serbs. They intermarried with their Orthodox neighbors and even kept that uniquely Serbian Orthodox religious custom, the *krsna slava*, which celebrates the patron saint of a family, not of an individual. The Catholic tombstone of Mato Vragolav (d. 1907) in Konavle tells the story:

> Owner of a large estate and lawyer
> By origin from Cavtat
> In his heart a Serb

Sometime in the course of the terrible 20th century, the words "in his heart a Serb" were deliberately effaced by a misguided Catholic, who had been indoctrinated into the Croatian nationalism that equates religion with ethnicity. The monument is cited by Djordje Ćapin, who documents even more outrageous attempts to forge false histories and destroy the past that cannot be falsified.

The Slavic tribes known as Serbs and Croats entered Roman Dalmatia sometime later, perhaps during the long reign of Heraclius (610-40), who asked for their help in his struggles with the Avars.[5] After some years of plundering the entire peninsula and destroying Risan, the major settlement on Boka Kotorska, the Avars eventually withdrew north of the Danube, but the Slavs had come to stay—in large parts of Greece, Macedonia, Thrace, and what is now Serbia and Dalmatia. Though the conquest of Greece did not represent a permanent or thoroughgoing ethnic transformation, from Macedonia to north of the Danube, the area became known to the Byzantines as "Sclavinia."

To gain a free hand for his wars against Persia, Heraclius sent tribute and family members as hostages to the Avar Khan. He also allied himself with the distant Khazars and the not-so distant Bulgars, who revolted against the Avar Khan and moved into the Balkans. The power struggle between Slavs and Avars was only settled, when Croats succeeded in freeing themselves from the Avars and moved to the northwest of the peninsula, while the Serbs chose to head south and east. These Serbs and Croats, although they may have been comparatively small in numbers, were able to dominate the earlier Slavic settlers, to whom they gave their respective names.

The First Serbs

Serbs, who left traces of their name behind in Germany and Poland, were among the first five Slavic peoples listed by name in the Russian *Story of the Past*. In the Balkans evidence of their early settlements has been found in much of what is now Serbia (including Kosovo), Bosnia, and Macedonia. The first explicit reference to permanent Serbian settlement in Montenegro goes back no farther than 822, when Ljudevit, the ruler of Posavina (the Sava river basin), after being attacked by the Franks, fled from the town of Sisak "to the Serbs who, people say, live in the greater part of Dalmatia."

We know all too little of these early Serbs. Like other Slavs, they were fair-skinned people with gray-blue eyes, herders and farmers rather than merchants, fond of battle but not yet able, at that early time, to accept the discipline and organization on which an effective army and a state are formed. The Avars and other Turkic tribes, who were actually on a lower level of social and cultural development, enforced a military discipline that explains the nomads' ability to dominate agricultural peoples who were more advanced.

Like most Slavic peoples at this period the Serbs were not yet organized into a state but were living in extended kin-groups (the *pleme* or clan) or organized in a larger confederation (*župa*) ruled by a župan. The *župa* was not so much a piece of territory as an alliance of kindreds united by ties of intermarriage and common experience. The clan has played an important role in Serbian social life, especially in more remote areas ethnic structure. Some of the clans gave their names to the regions where they settled, and while the shifts and fissions of the clans have resulted in confusion through the centuries, clan traditions continue to play a part in Montenegrin life down to the present.

The Threatened Empire of the East

The Serbs, like other Slavs, were brave fighters, but their loose social and political organization was ill designed to confront the military machines of the Huns and Turkic peoples whose primary business was war, and Balkan Serbs were hard-pressed in the sixth century by the Avars and after 680 by the Bulgars, a people of mixed Slavic and Turkic origin—to say nothing of the continuing Byzantine threat. Emperor Constans II had apparently forced the Slavs of Sclavinia (in 658) to acknowledge Byzantine suzerainty, and near the end of the eighth century, the empire reasserted control over Greece and successfully re-hellenized the Peloponnese. Nonetheless, the seventh and eighth centuries were a period of great troubles for the Byzantine Empire, which made it easier for the Slavic peoples (including the increasingly Slavicized Bulgars) to consolidate their foothold in the Balkans.

In the East, the Arabs, now that they were converted to a militant religion, kept the Byzantines busy just staying alive, while internally the empire was wracked by the deadly struggle between iconoclasts and iconodoules (the opponents and supporters of religious images). They also had to meet a rising challenge to their supremacy from the Frankish king, Charles the Great, crowned emperor in Rome in 800. Not content with an empire that included France, Germany, Austria, and Italy, Charlemagne was also stretching his hands out to the Istrian coast (part of today's northwestern Croatia).

The great threat to Byzantine control of the Balkans came first from the Bulgars, who were able to establish a largely Slavic kingdom at the backdoor of Constantinople, and in the early eighth century the Bulgar Khan Tervel even received the title Caesar, honored and enthroned beside the emperor Justinian II in Constantinople. However, the Bulgarian advance did not go unopposed. After decades of misrule by women and their puppets, the empire found a good ruler in Nicephorus I (802-11), who had to face an insurgent Bulgarian kingdom led by the redoubtable Krum, but after a series of brilliant victories, Nicephorus was defeated and slain, and his skull was turned into a goblet that Krum used at his gaudy feasts. Though Krum died (like Attila) of a cerebral hemorrhage in 814, the Bulgarians continued to attack the Empire, which, though it was freed from the threat in the East posed by the great Caliph Haroun al Rashid, had to undergo another destructive and divisive round of iconoclasm under Leo V.

In the mid-ninth century, too, the growing tensions with the Roman Church reached a crisis under Patriarch Photius, a fine scholar whose appointment the Pope (Nicholas I) decided to challenge as a means of asserting the church's universal power. At the height of the conflict, however, the Byzantine throne was seized by Basil the Macedonian, who established the most successful dynasty in the long history of the Eastern Empire. It was under the Macedonians that the Byzantines broke the power of the Bulgars (who were trying to play Rome against Constantinople, a common game of Balkan Slavs) and reestablished control of the Balkans.

The primary evidence for coastal Serbia in this period is the *Chronicle*, written in the 12th century by a Latin priest in Duklja ("Pop Dukljanin"). Although the chronology is unreliable, and much of the information apocryphal at best, the *Chronicle* does preserve authentic traditions, especially from the 10th century onward.

Along the coast the Serbs settled principally in four territories. *Neretva* lay between the Cetina and Neretva rivers. This district was sometime called Pagania, or Pagan-land, because it was home to unbaptized Serbs, who engaged in piracy. The Neretljani alternated between fighting Arab pirate fleets and raiding the shipping of the Venetian Republic.

When, in 870, the pirates of Neretva seized ambassadors returning from Constantinople to Rome, Pope Adrian II complained bitterly to Emperor Basil I, who liberated the ambassadors and punished the Neretljani so severely that other Serb principalities acknowledged Byzantine suzerainty. The pirates did not mend their ways, however, for many years, and the chronicles of the period record wars and treaties between Venice and Neretva. In 840, Venetians campaigned successfully against the pirates, but in 887 the Neretljani defeated Doge Pietro Candiano, who was killed in the battle, and in 948 an exasperated Venice not only gave up all claims for tribute from the Serbs but even agreed to pay them an annual subsidy.[6]

Serbs also settled in Hercegovina, in areas known as *Zahumlje* (or Hum or Humska zemlja), which lay between the Neretva River and Dubrovnik, and in Travunija, the territory centered in Trebinje, which stretched from Dubrovnik to Kotor (ancient Catarum) and up to the mountains. Greeks and Latins had both settled the region, but Greeks were predominant in Boka, and Kotor was at least nominally under the authority of Byzantium. By the ninth century, however, the Slavs were beginning to assert themselves, and in the late 1860's, it was Slavs, primarily, who resisted an Arab attack, and in the rebuilding of Kotor, the Slavs took the lead, making Kotor an eventually Slavic town. Kotor was to become a free city under first Byzantine, then Nemanjić rule.

The region that gave birth to the first Serbian state in what was to become Montenegro was Duklja (usually known as Zeta from the 12th century on), which extended from Kotor south to Bar, Ulcinj, and Lješ down to Dyracchium (Durazzo, modern Drač). West from the Lake of Scutari, the border continued along the Zeta River to the Piva River (in eastern Hercegovina). In speaking of Serbs in Montenegro and Dalmatia as if they were separate from other Balkan Serbs, it is important to bear in mind that the opposite is actually the case. Rising Serbian states, whether in the West or the East, aimed at uniting all the Serbs. Local rebellions in Zeta or Raška are less an expression of regional patriotism than a play for power.

Raška and Duklja

Throughout the eighth and ninth centuries, Serbian tribes and communities were coalescing into larger alliances, if only for the purposes of defense. Eventually a strong leader would emerge, making himself Veliki Župan (or Great Župan) and claiming allegiance from other župans within a region. In the areas of eastern and southern Serbia later known as Raška, Veliki Župan Vlastimir Vladislavić, said to have been the great-grandson of the first known Serbian ruler Višeslav, succeeded (in roughly 850) in uniting the Serbian tribes against the Bulgars, who were constantly seeking to extend their empire over the Serbs. Even at this early date, Vlastimir must have had wider territorial ambitions, since he made a dynastic alliance with the prince of Travunia (Trebinje), whose daughter he married.

Bulgars were anxious to block these first efforts at uniting the Serbs. After Vlastimir's death, he was succeeded by his son Mutimir, who decisively defeated the Bulgars and temporarily stopped their incursions into Serb territory. Mutimir was followed (after his son's brief reign) by his nephew, Petar Gojniković (892-917), who bowed to the necessity of making an alliance with the more distant enemy in Constantinople in order to defeat one closer at hand, namely, the expanding power of the Bulgarian Empire. Gojniković acknowledged the authority of Constantinople and succeeded in joining Neretva with Raška—despite the opposition put up by the ruler of Zahumlje and Duklja, Mihailo Višević, who was himself attempting to create a unified state out of the Serbian lands that lay along the coast.

The competing ambitions of the rulers of Raška and Duklja led to an inevitable conflict between the two rising Serb states. Both Mihailo and Petar were vassals of the Byzantine emperor, but the ruler of Zahumlje and Duklja broke with the empire to make an alliance with the Bulgarian Tsar Simeon. Mihailo eventually gained control of Neretva, but at the price of halting the unification of the Serbs.

Eventually, Byzantine diplomacy brought Mihailo back into the fold, and he was made consul and patrician of the empire and given authority over Kotor and Dubrovnik. To orient his people toward the East and away from the West, he also established a new bishopric in Ras (in southern Serbia). This Byzantine orientation, however, did not prevent him from joining forces with Tomislav, the ruler of Croatia, in a struggle with Constantinople.

The Bulgars did succeed in reestablishing their rule over the eastern Serbs (924-27), and the Tsar Simeon, who divided up Serbian territories the better to rule the people, practiced abominable cruelties against the Serbs. Časlav Klonimirović, a great-grandson of Vlastimir, eventually unified the Serbs of the region to defeat the Bulgars. Raised in Preslav (the Bulgar capital) as the Bulgarian candidate for the Serbian throne, Časlav was able to liberate his people and strike a deal with Emperor Romanus I. The death of Mihailo Višević removed Duklja (albeit briefly) from the competition for power, enabling Časlav to form the first united Serb state covering western Serbia, eastern Bosnia and Hercegovina. Časlav's state was the first to bear the name "Serbia."

Although Serb rulers on the coast acknowledged the authority of Časlav, they remained virtually independent. Neretva, for example, had never abandoned piracy, and the Neretljani continued to fight the Venetians, but this was a side-show compared with the larger struggle. After a long and successful reign in which he aligned the Serbs increasingly toward Constantinople and the Orthodox Church, Časlav died in 960 resisting a Magyar invasion. After his death, his union of Serbs dissolved into feuding fragments, and the ruling family of Višeslav disappeared.

The Kingdom of Zeta

Along the coast (or Primorje, as it is still known), Duklja not only seceded from the rest of Serbia but also disintegrated (like Raška) into feuding clans and warlords, leaving the Bulgars and Byzantines to battle for supremacy over Serbia and Macedonia. However, within a few decades of Časlav's death, Jovan Vladimir came to power in Duklja and ruled, until 1016, from his capital in Scutari. Vladimir took advantage of the troubles in the Bulgarian state in Macedonia, and in a bid for independence he refused to recognize the authority of Tsar Samuel. The Serbs were defeated, and Samuel captured Duklja and imprisoned Vladimir in Struga. The two were reconciled, however, and Vladimir married the tsar's daughter and, as a dowry, he received Duklja and Trebinje, which he ruled in peace, staying clear of the struggle between Constantinople and the Bulgars that ended in Samuel's disastrous defeat.

There is a more romantic legend concerning the courtship of Vladimir and the Bulgarian princess. The pious Princess Kosara took pity on the Serb prisoner, and when pity turned to love, she persuaded her father to make him the tsar's son-in-law, saying she would rather die than accept another man.[7] After Samuel's defeat and death, his nephew Vladislav invited Vladimir to a conference in Struga and had him killed as he was leaving church. According to the legend preserved in the *Duklja Chronicle*, Kosara unsuccessfully tried to warn her husband against her cousin's plot. The grave of Vladimir and Kosara lies in Scutari, and the Orthodox Church has made him a saint. For centuries, Orthodox Serbs and even Albanian Muslims have made annual pilgrimages to his shrine.

During Vladimir's reign, the pirates of Neretva were back in business, harassing the people of the islands and the Dalmatian coast. Exasperated by the raiding, the local inhabitants swore allegiance to Venice, and in the closing years of the tenth century, the Doge Pietro Orsoleo II sailed with a strong fleet to Dalmatia, where most of the islands loyal to Neretva—with the exception of Hvar and Korčula—surrendered. Korčula, which lacked the resources to withstand a siege, gave in, but Hvar held out through a long and bloody fight until the Venetians captured the island. They followed up their success by invading Neretva itself, compelling the Neretljani to give up their lucrative business and to renounce the subsidy they had been receiving from Venice. The 160-year-old conflict was over, and the Doge assumed the title "Dux Dalmatiae"—a claim the Venetians could not yet enforce south of the Neretva.

After Vladimir's death in 1016, strife was created in Duklja over the throne, a struggle in which Samuel's heir Vladislav attempted to involve himself, albeit without much success. Vladimir's uncle, as eldest in the family, tried to assert his right to succeed, but he was killed by the people of Kotor, whom he had asked to transport his army. Kotor proclaimed its independence, though under the suzerainty of Constantinople. For in fact, Byzantine power in the Balkans was at its height under Emperor Basil II, named "the Bulgar-slayer" after he inflicted a terrifying defeat and punishment upon Samuel's army. The defeated Bulgars were all blinded, except the one man in a hundred who was left with one eye so that he could guide the army back to the grief-stricken ruler. However, after Basil's death in 1025, Byzantine power steadily declined, giving an opportunity to the Serbs to regroup and rebuild.

Within ten years of Basil's death, Stefan Vojislav (1035-51) had become sole ruler of Duklja, which he made independent of the empire.

Vojislav had initially tried to take advantage of the disturbances that broke out after the death of Basil II, but his uprising failed, and he was captured and imprisoned in Constantinople, where he observed the weakness of the Byzantine Empire. Breaking out of prison, he returned to Duklja in 1040 and fomented another uprising. When an imperial treasure ship was wrecked upon the coast, Vojislav seized the money and defied the empire. Emperor Constantine IX Monomachos, once he had come to the throne and consolidated his authority, sent a large army to retake the region. The Byzantine campaign was supported by his local vassals, the Serbian rulers of Raška, Bosnia, and Zahumlje, who attacked Duklja from the north. Vojislav chose to face his most powerful adversary first, and he trapped the Byzantine army in a pass near Bar. The troops of Zeta rolled down rocks from the cliffs upon the imperial soldiers, and in the course of the night attack, the panicked Byzantine troops were routed by the Serbs (in 1042). This may be the first recorded instance of a Montenegrin ruler luring a superior army into the mountains in order to mount a surprise attack, but it was a pattern that would be repeated regularly for almost a thousand years.[8]

Vojislav then sent his son Gojislav north to fight the army led by Knez (Prince) Ljutovid of Zahumlje, who had seized Trebinje. Ljutovid would not agree to a proposed treaty, but when his Serbian soldiers refused to fight their brothers, he determined to keep faith with the emperor, challenged Gojislav and a companion to a duel with himself and a second. Wounded in the duel, Ljutovid withdrew, and Vojislav followed up his victory by uniting Duklja with Raška and Bosnia, which revolted from the empire.

Vojislav wanted to establish a Serbian kingdom independent of both Byzantium and Rome. This required a degree of adroit maneuvering. When Dabral, the archbishop of Bar, convoked a council of bishops, a high wind came up and sank the boat in which the bishops of Bar, Ulcinj, and Kotor were traveling, drowning the prelates. This "fortunate" accident gave Vojislav the opportunity to establish an independent church. Though the final schism between East and West would not take place until 1054, coastal Dalmatia was under the jurisdiction of the Pope, and the corrupt Pope Benedict IX, seeing the chance to make headway, transferred the lapsed bishopric of Duklja (a town by then in ruins) to Bar. This action would be the source of endless friction between Dubrovnik and Bar.

Upon his death, Stefan Vojislav left five sons to rule his principality, but after a few years his son Mihailo Vojislavljević (1051?-1081) made himself sole ruler and assumed the title of king. He quickly reestablished peace with the Byzantine emperor and forced Raška, which had revolted, back into submission. When an uprising of Macedonian Slavs broke out under Djordje Vojteh (1072), Mihailo sent his son Konstantin Bodin to lead the insurgents. Defeating the Byzantine army near Prizren, he was proclaimed the new Bulgarian tsar by the local Slavic leaders. After several initial victories, Bodin was defeated in Kosovo and sent as prisoner to Antioch. The rebellious Slavs were forced back under Byzantine rule. Nonetheless, Mihailo was able to extend his authority into Raška, which he put under the control of another son Petrislav.

It was during Mihailo's reign that the Byzantine world was shaken by waves of raiding Russians, Magyars, and Pechenegs (a Turkish tribe from north of the Danube), and Seljuk Turks. At Manzikert (in Armenia) in 1071, Turks annihilated the Byzantine army and captured the Emperor Romanus. During the same period, the Normans were seizing Southern Italy under the pretext of helping the Italians in their struggle to resist Byzantine control. Bari fell to Robert Guiscard in the same year as the Manzikert catastrophe. Mihailo took advantage of the disorders, not only to secure the release of his son Bodin (whether by bribery or by diplomacy) but also to assert the independence of Duklja, which becomes known as Zeta (a name formerly applied to one župa within Duklja).

The schism between the eastern and western branches of Christendom afforded Mihailo another opportunity to increase his independence. He appealed to Pope Gregory VII, who recognized him as king in exchange for the king's submission to Rome. Submission to Rome cannot have been entirely satisfactory, since it had been decreed, at a council held in Split not long before the schism, that the Slavonic language was not to be used in the Catholic liturgy, and we hear of resistance to the Latinization of the church.

Konstantin Bodin, the last of the important rulers of Zeta before the rise of the Nemanjići, succeeded to the throne on his father's death in 1081, though probably not without a dynastic struggle within the ruling family. Bodin continued his father's policy, relying on Rome and the Normans while protesting his loyalty to Constantinople, which still exercised suzerainty over Bosnia and Raška. In the struggle between the Normans and the Byzantines over Dyrrachium, Bodin's decision to withdraw his troops at a critical moment contributed to the emperor's defeat, and when Emperor Alexius Komnenos finally did succeed in driving the Normans out of Albania, he was able to turn his attention to Bodin.

In the interim, however, while Alexius was distracted with the defense of the empire, Bodin expanded his power to include Bosnia and Raška, and he egged on Vukan (probably the son of his half-brother Petrislav), whom he had made Veliki Župan of Raška, to attack Byzantine territory in Kosovo but with a force inadequate to resist the emperor. The treaty struck in 1094 between the empire and Raška confirmed Vukan in his possessions, but the Serbs agreed to attempt no future advances. The Pope, to reward Bodin for his loyalty (Bodin had supported the Pope against the anti-pope Clement), raised the bishopric of Bar to the rank of archbishopric and designated the archbishop as primate of Serbia.

The Emperor Alexius was soon to face a far greater threat to his empire than the Kingdom of Zeta. In 1095 Pope Urban VII had proclaimed a crusade to rescue the Holy Land from the infidels. By the spring of 1096, a horde of volunteers was pillaging the district around Belgrade. The armies of crusaders followed soon afterward, and one of the leaders, Raymond of Toulouse, stopped in Dalmatia and conversed with Bodin, "King of Dalmatia."

After the death of Bodin, the struggles for the throne broke out again, lasting for several decades. During the same period the Magyars made their way into Croatia and Dalmatia and began their long-term push toward domination of the Balkans. Croatia was annexed to the Hungarian crown in 1102, and the Hungarians began occupying cities along the Dalmatian coast. Any hopes that might have been cherished for a Serbian kingdom headquartered in Zeta perished in battles with Hungarians and Byzantines and in the suicidal infighting among claimants to Bodin's throne.

If the rulers of Zeta had been aiming at the establishment of an independent power-base in Montenegro, their failure was of little consequence for the future. However, it seems clear that, on the contrary, their goal was the unification of the Serbian peoples under a single ruler. While it is too much, perhaps, to describe the loose, feudal union of Raška and Zeta, each with its own hereditary župans, as a state, the broader objective of Serbian leaders can be seen in the dynastic marriages that had been made between Raška and Zeta and from Zeta's willingness to participate in the wider Serbian struggle against both Bulgars and Byzantium. The rival leaders of Zeta and Raška had to have been aware of the urgent necessity of founding a general Serbian state, strong enough and large enough to defend the Serbs from their enemies. Little Zeta, even if a strong leader had succeeded Bodin, could never have survived for very long on its own.

In the brief history of Zeta, the Serbs of Montenegro had been forced to make obeisance to the Pope, and her rulers had tried, not always successfully, to play the great powers of Italy against the Byzantine Empire. Caught between the Magyars and Croats to the North, the Normans and Venetians across the Adriatic, and the resurgent authority of the empire under the competent Komnenos dynasty, the rulers of Zeta could only defend their people and interests as part of a more powerful Serbian kingdom.

Notes

The best narrative account of the Byzantine period remains Gibbon's *Decline and Fall*, especially the edition edited and annotated by J.B. Bury who frequently corrects Gibbon's errors and prejudices, *e.g.* against the Serbs, whom he only deigns to mention as "barbarians," who should not have been allowed to involve themselves in the affairs of civilized men. Of more recent historians available in English, Ostrogorsky had, perhaps, the greatest interest and deepest knowledge

1. Cf. Vasiliev, vol. I, p. 110. Procopius describes annual raiding parties in reign of Justinian.

2. Procopius, *Bellum Gothicum* VII. 14.22.

3. Procopius VII.40.7-8.

4. The earliest Slavic settlement, dated to the mid fifth century, was on the Drina River near the modern Musići. Slavs gradually turned from raiders into settlers. Irma Cremošnik, "Istraživanja u Musićima žabljaku i prvi nalaz najstarijih slovenskih naselja kod nas," *Glasnik zemaljskog muzeja*, XXV (Sarajevo, 1970), pp. 45-111.

5. There is controversy over the dates and circumstances. Emperor Constantine VII Porphyrogenius, *De administrando imperio* 20-36 gives detailed account of Serbs and Croats; cf. Ostrogorsky 104-5.

6. Popović, pp. 24-5.

7. Pop Dukljanin, XXXVI.

8. Temperly, p. 35.

9. Vojislav was known to the Priest of Duklja as Dobroslav.

THE SERBIAN GOLDEN AGE

In the early decades of the 12th century, Serbian prospects were dim. Their fragmenting kingdoms, harassed by the Magyars in the north, were facing a threat to their very existence in a reviving Byzantine Empire, which was under the competent rulers of the Komnenos family. The empire not only exercised theoretical suzerainty over the Serbs of Raška and Zeta but demanded a tribute of 2,000 soldiers for Constantinople's European campaigns and 500 for service in Asian wars.

On the death of Vukan about 1122, his son Uroš came to power in Raška with the support of the Magyars. The attempts of Uroš I and his son Uroš II to assert authority over Zeta brought the rulers of Raška into conflict with Byzantium. In alliance with the Magyars, Uroš II attacked the Emperor Manuel, who followed up his victory by conquering the Hungarians in Bosnia. Uroš II was deposed twice by Byzantine power and replaced by his brother Desa. By 1162, Manuel had reconquered all the Serb lands, including Bosnia, and divided them up among four brothers: Tihomir, Stracimir, Miroslav, and Stefan Nemanja. The brothers were sons of Zavid, who was *probably* a son of Uroš I. Zavid is said to have fled to Zeta, where his son Nemanja was born in 1122. It is a point worth underscoring that this Nemanja, who was to resurrect the hopes of Serbian independence, had ancestral roots in both Raška and Zeta.[1]

The Emperor obviously expected the brothers to rule their weakened fiefdoms in allegiance to Byzantium and to defend the empire from the Magyars. Though he was motivated by no good will toward the Serbs, Manuel helped, in a real sense, to create the first Serbian kingdom by uniting the Orthodox Serbs against the Hungarians, who by 1153 had conquered Croatia and much of Dalmatia.

According to a biography written by his son, Nemanja had been born in Zeta and baptized Catholic, but he was subsequently re-baptized by an Orthodox priest. Nemanja received the smallest territorial share of Manuel's gift (around Toplica, in southern Serbia), but he made himself so popular that his brothers, sensing danger, conspired against him. Imprisoned by Tihomir, Nemanja (according to the story told by his son Stefan) prayed to St. George, who assisted him to escape and later aided him in his battles. Nemanja emerged victorious from the family struggle, and, with Manuel's support, he displaced his brother Tihomir as Veliki Župan; routed (in 1170) the Byzantine army, which had invaded Kosovo to restore Tihomir as a loyal imperial vassal; and, conquering Kosovo, northern Macedonia, and the northeastern part of the Morava River valley, laid the foundations of a unified Serbian commonwealth.

Nemanja followed up his victory by expelling King Radoslav of Zeta and annexing Trebinje, Zahumlje, Neretva, and Zeta itself, which he turned over to his son Vukan. For the next 200 years, Zeta existed mainly as a part—albeit an autonomous and sometimes virtually independent part—of the kingdom (and later the empire) created by the Nemanjić dynasty. Along the Adriatic, the Veliki Župan also recaptured Skadar, Bar, Budva, Ulcinj, and other towns from the empire and fortified Kotor, where he displayed his good taste as well as a strategic sense by building a palace for himself.

Dubrovnik, where Radoslav had taken refuge, proved to be a thorn in the side of Nemanja and his successors, and when the commercial republic quarreled with Kotor over questions of church authority, Nemanja went to war on behalf of Kotor—and also, apparently, to reduce the burdensome tariffs imposed by Dubrovnik. Part of the dispute was over ecclesiastical jurisdiction. Dubrovnik was jealous of Bar, which the pope had made an archbishopric in 1089, but in 1142, after years of plotting and complaining, Dubrovnik persuaded the pope to degrade Bar. When Nemanja took over Bar, the bishop, highly resentful of Dubrovnik, acquired a powerful ally. Nemanja may have briefly taken Dubrovnik but was unable to hold it. Peace was eventually reached on condition of free trade for Nemanja's subjects. Disputes between Serbs and Ragusans were a constant source of friction, and according to the treaty, the city had to set up impartial courts consisting of equal numbers of each group.

Nemanja was a wily diplomatist, who, in his search for an ally against the Byzantine empire, made compacts first with Venice and then with Friedrich Barbarossa, who was preparing to lead a crusade. The Serb ruler supplied the army of the German emperor, whom he met at Niš in 1189. The death of Barbarossa allowed the Byzantine Emperor Issac Angelos to strike back at Nemanja, whom he defeated, though the two rulers struck a marriage alliance between Nemanja's second son and Eudokia, the daughter of Emperor Alexios III. In matters of religion, Nemanja also drew closer to Constantinople. He opted for the Orthodox religion, probably in expectation of founding a national church, and he took the first steps toward eliminating the Bogomil heresy. His youngest son Rastko became a monk and adopted the name Sava (after the Cappadocian Saint Sabbas).

In creating a stable and powerful Serbian state, Nemanja and his successors did not have to face strong competition from Byzantium, whose strength, weakened by poor leadership and challenged by both Arabs and Crusaders, was on the wane in the closing decades of the 12th century. The Fourth Crusade, in which the "Franks" chose to conquer Christian Constantinople rather than to attack the more dangerous Muslims, put what was left of the empire into the greedy and incompetent hands of the French nobility, and although the capture of Constantinople meant that even a revived Byzantine Empire would inevitably fall prey to the Turks, it did afford the Nemanjić rulers some breathing space in which to consolidate their kingdom.

Ascent to Glory

In 1196, Nemanja abdicated in favor of his second son, Stefan. Vukan was supposed to be content with being "Great Prince" of Zeta, though he revealed his ambition even before his father's abdication by styling himself "King." Nemanja became a monk and, taking the name Simeon, went first to live in Studenica monastery, which he had founded, and then to Mt. Athos to join his son Sava at the Hilandar monastery. Vukan did not accept his younger brother's preferment with good grace and intrigued with the Pope to have himself recognized as king—on the usual terms. Not to be outdone, Stefan asked the Pope to recognize his own position as king. This was a good opportunity to counter the growing strength of the Orthodox Church among the Serbs, and the Pope urged King Emeric of Hungary to conquer the Serbs and deliver them to the Catholic Church. With Hungarian and papal support, Vukan installed himself as ruler, but upon the withdrawal of the Hungarians, Vukan realized the dangerous position in which he had placed himself. Stefan was reinstated, and Vukan went back to Zeta. The two brothers were reconciled by their younger brother, Sava, who is the founder of the Serbian Church.

Vukan's rule in Zeta has sometimes been treated as an example of Zetan nationalism, but such a grandiose political conception is an anachronism:

Both Raška and Zeta were populated by Serbs. But the loyalty of most people then was to a far more local unit than a region like Zeta. It was to a village, or possibly to a county or to a family . . . Those Zetan nobles who supported Vukan . . . surely did so for they personal advantages they saw in the policy, and not because of any Zetan consciousness.[2]

Vukan abdicated the throne of Zeta in favor of his son Djuradj, who maintained the family feud within the Nemanjić dynasty and put Zeta under the protection of Venice, though by 1216 Stefan had wrested control, and the Nemanjić kings retained power over Zeta until Dušan's death.[3]

Stefan's first wife was a member of the Byzantine imperial family, but when he caught her in adultery, he sent her back to her imperial relatives with only one dress. For his second wife, he looked westward to Venice and married the granddaughter of Doge Enrico Dandolo. The king's brother Sava, perhaps out of dissatisfaction with the westward tilt of the kingdom, left for two years, but he returned to put the Serbian Orthodox Church on a firm foundation. During this period of the Latin occupation of Constantinople, the Serbian Church was subject to the bishop of

Ohrid, which lay within the domain of the "empire" in Nicaea. By playing upon the rivalry between the two claimants to the Byzantine Empire, Sava was able to secure an autocephalous status for his Church. In 1219 Sava became the first Serbian Orthodox archbishop, and he quickly got rid of Greek bishops and reorganized the Church into probably ten dioceses. He also formalized the canon law of the Serbian

St. Sava and St. Simeon, Monastery of Morača

Church and arranged for the Greek theological and ecclesiastical works to be translated.

Although Stefan had received coronation from a papal legate in exchange for a promise to reestablish the Catholic Church among the Serbs, Sava is believed to have crowned his brother in a Serbian ceremony in 1220, though the second crowning is often disputed.

The breach between Raška and Zeta was eventually healed, though under Radoslav (the son of Stefan I), Vukan's son Djuradj was back in Zeta ruling as a prince. Following the tradition established by Nemanja, Zeta was often governed by the son or brother of the Serbian king. When, for example, Stefan Vladislav was deposed by the National Assembly (Skupstina) in 1242 in favor of his brother, Stefan Uroš I "the Great," Vladislav went to Dubrovnik, where he was eventually appointed governor of Zeta.

Zeta made continued progress under Nemanja's successors, who laid roads within the region, opened mines, and assisted in the commercial development of coastal towns. Uroš I (1243-76), realizing the dangers inherent in a decentralized and feudal system, eliminated the names of Zeta and Hum and called himself "King of all Serbian lands and the coast." Uroš's son Dragutin drove his father from the throne and appointed his mother, Jelena of Anjou, as ruler of Zeta. Jelena strove to improve relations between the Serbian state and the coastal towns, which were predominantly Roman or Greek. These towns, though they paid tribute and acknowledged the authority of the Serbian king, were free to administer their own affairs without interference.

By playing off Serbs against Hungarians and Venetians and Byzantines, these coastal towns were able to increase their autonomy. In 1242, a conflict between Split and Trogir had the disastrous result of Hungarian intervention. Bela IV occupied the towns and then seized Bosnia. Uroš I had also had troubles with Dubrovnik, which had given his brother refuge. To secure its independence, Dubrovnik made alliances with both Bulgaria and Hungarian-dominated Hum. In 1253, after a decade of provocations, Uroš I decided to crack down and exert a more direct control over Dubrovnik, whose location gave it an economic stranglehold over Raška. After defeating Dubrovnik and its allies and annexing Hum to his kingdom, Uroš was able to turn his attention to expanding into Macedonia.

Contests over the Serbian throne invited foreign interventions into Serbian affairs and also provided a pretext for separatist uprisings, and not only in Zeta, where impatient heirs to the throne were able to play upon the separatist ambitions of the local nobility. When Uroš I was overthrown by Dragutin, his son relied on Hungarian help, though his treachery may have later contributed to the decision to depose him in favor of his brother Stefan Uroš II Milutin, who had been in charge of Zeta, Hum, and Trebinje. Dragutin's willingness to abdicate was partly inspired by a hunting accident, which he interpreted as an evil omen. Nonetheless, the former king remained a powerful political figure among the Serbs, with strong ties to the West — Hungary in particular — and the marriage of his daughter to Stjepan Kotroman, Ban of Bosnia, helped to bring Bosnia into closer relations with the Serbian kingdom.

Dragutin's brother and successor, King Stefan Uroš II Milutin, had his own family problems. When he failed to follow up on his defeat of the Byzantines in Macedonia, much of the Serb nobility (especially in Zeta, where his son Stefan was ruling) rose up in 1314 to support Stefan's bid to supplant his father. Although Stefan Dečanski (as Milutin's son was later known, from the monastery he founded) was eventually to succeed Milutin in 1321, he was defeated, blinded, and sent in chains, with his two sons Dušan and Dušica, to Constantinople, while his younger brother Constantine was invested with the administration of Zeta.

Milutin has been blamed by historians for his harshness against his son and for lack of initiative against Byzantium. It should be pointed out, however, that consolidation of the Serbian kingdom was a far more urgent task than the conquest of Byzantine territory. If the Serbs and Greeks had succeeded in standing together peacefully throughout the 14th century, they would have had a better chance of resisting the Turks. The unity of the Serbs in Milutin's time is apparent from his foundation of the Monastery of St. Nicholas on Vranjina Mountain (in modern Montenegro). Although the monastery was built in an area inhabited by Latins, Albanians, Vlachs, and Serbs, the charter refers explicitly to Serbs in the ethnic sense.[4] When the strong and competent Milutin died, his son Stefan Uroš III Dečanski came to power, but there must have been doubts about his abilities. Rebellions broke out, and Zahumlje (Hercegovina) broke free, cutting off access to the sea, and the king took (or was forced to take) his 14-year-old son Dušan as a junior partner ruling over Zeta. Stefan Dečanski intervened in a dynastic struggle over the empire and managed to secure Prilep, which was later famous as the stronghold of Marko Kraljević.

Unlike his son, the king was a peace-loving ruler who preferred negotiation to war. With Dušan's help, he decisively defeated and subdued the Bulgarians, but he may not have been aggressive enough for his vojovode, who persuaded his son (according to Dušan later) that the king was plotting against his life. In rebelling against his father, Dušan used the same excuse that the king had failed to press his advantages against his Greek relations in Constantinople. The two eventually reached an agreement, though disgruntled Zetan noblemen murdered Dečanski, for which they were punished severely by Dušan.

The landed nobility of Zeta and Albanian landed gentry, who had supported the plot, regarded Dušan's reconciliation with his father as an act of betrayal, and at the beginning of his reign a rebellion broke out, headed by Bogoja, who possessed lands in Zeta, and the Albanian Dimitrije Suma. They were aided, apparently, by Dušan's stepmother, the widow of Stefan Dečanski. Dušan quelled the rebellion and went on, taking over Macedonia and large parts of Greece and Albania, to make himself tsar over an empire of Serbs, Romans (Greeks), Bulgars, and Albanians.

Emperor Dušan Nemanjić

Dušan's title exceeded reality. Much of Greece lay within Byzantine control, and south-central Albania at this time (1269-1368) was controlled by Charles of Anjou and his descendants. Their control could only be exercised rather loosely over a number of powerful families: the Musachi, who supported Byzantium against the Serbs; the Topia, who supported the Angevin interests (the great Karlo Topia was the son of an illegitimate daughter of the Angevin king of Naples); and the Serbian Balšići. Distracted by a conflict with Hungary, Dušan died (1355) before his plans to conquer the last vestiges of the Byzantine Empire could mature.

Decline and Fall

Tsar Dušan has always been regarded as among the greatest of Serb rulers, and deservedly so. However, with the benefit of historical hindsight, he can be accused of one of the two classic mistakes made by Serb leaders: He attempted the creation of a multiethnic state, whose inherent instability made it prey to internal dissension and open to attack from abroad. Dušan's excessive ambition led naturally to the other classic error of Serb leaders: showing disunity in the face of powerful enemies. During the reign of his son and untalented successor, Tsar Uroš "Nejaki" (the weak or immature—he was only 18 when his father died), Dušan's empire began to succumb to foreign shocks administered by the Turks and to crumble from within.

In the disordered years of Uroš's misrule, the landed gentry of Zeta were among those who took the lead in dismembering the Serbian state, but they were hardly the only contenders. Uroš's uncle, after losing Thessaly, tried to displace his nephew, but, defeated in Zeta, he returned to his province and wrested control. During the same period, the king of Hungary took Belgrade. Throughout the Serb lands, local potentates rose up to dispute power both with Uroš and with each other, and the result was chaos and lawlessness. Although Lazar Hrebeljanović and Vuk Branković remained loyal, Nikola Altomanović took much of southern Hum and Trebinje, and in the south, the Mrnjavčevići expanded their territories and became independent.

Vukašin Mrnjavčević, whose family came from Hum, made himself virtual ruler of Macedonia. The troubles of those days are brilliantly (if inaccurately) conveyed in a folk poem recorded in Kolašin (in "old Hercegovina," now a part of Montenegro) during the 19th century. The arrogant Mrnjavčević (as they are called), each of whom claims the throne for himself, have terrorized the young Uroš, and when the choice is left up to Vukašin's son Marko, the prince supports the legitimate heir—setting an example that, if the other princes had followed, it would have averted the disaster of Kosovo. It is Marko's mother who gives the moral: "Never speak false either for your father or your uncles, but speak the truth for the sake of the true God. Better to lose your head than imperil your soul."

In 1366, Vukašin had himself proclaimed king and repudiated the canonical legality of the Serbian patriarch. Vukašin apparently wished to strengthen the ties with the declining Byzantine Empire for a common defense of the Balkans against the Ottoman Turks, who had already established a capital at Adrianople. Unsupported by the shortsighted Western powers, Vukašin and his brothers faced the Turks on the banks of the Marica River (near Černomen) in September 1371. The annihilation of the Mrnjavčevići's army—the Serb disaster, as it is called—opened the way for future Turkish invasions, and even in the short term, one after another of the fragmented Serbian states fell to the Turks. Vukašin's son, though forced by necessity to become a Turkish vassal, lived on as the most popular of Serbian folk heroes.

The king of Hungary, meanwhile, pursued his designs on Bosnia, where King Tvrtko ruled over a people divided—then as now—by religious differences among Catholics, Orthodox, and (in Tvrtko's time) Bogomils. Tvrtko had already taken over, by agreement with Venice, much of Dalmatia, and he added Hum to his expanding territory. In order to consolidate his power on the coast, Tvrtko began construction of Novi (later Herceg-Novi) at the mouth of the Gulf of Kotor in order to challenge the commercial monopoly exercised by Dubrovnik.

Upon the death of Uroš in 1371, three separate Serbian centers of power were in operation: Serbia and Kosovo under Lazar, Zeta under the Balšić family, and Bosnia, ruled by King Tvrtko, who was ready to make good his claim (as King Dragutin's great-grandson) to the Serbian throne and to carry out a plan for uniting eastern and western Serbs. Unexpectedly, Tvrtko was not directly opposed by Knez Lazar Hrebeljanović, who had become, after defeating his rival Nikola Altomanović, the *de facto* ruler of Raška. Although he was never crowned emperor, Prince Lazar was called tsar in the folk tradition, and in his reign (1371-89), he showed himself a competent and patriotic ruler. To reestablish stability, he reconciled the Serbian Church with Constantinople and had the anathema lifted, and to give his rule greater legitimacy, he attached himself to the Nemanjić tradition by marrying Milica, the daughter of Vlatko (known in the traditional Kosovo songs as old Jug-Bogdan), a descendant of Vukan, the eldest son of Stefan Nemanja.

His wise decision to cooperate, rather than contend, with King Tvrtko of Bosnia brought success within the realm of probability, which makes his death in battle with the Turks at Kosovo in 1389 a tragic disaster for the Serbs. Though Kosovo was closer to a drawn battle than a Turkish victory, the Turks were able to take advantage of the Serbs' demoralization by seizing the former Serb capital Skoplje in 1392 and Skadar in 1393.

Lazar's widow and her son Stefan Lazarević were obliged to swear fealty to the sultan, an oath they were careful to maintain throughout their lives. Their prudence, unheroic as it might appear, gave the Serbs a breathing space, especially when the Turks took to fighting among themselves. At Ankyra in 1402, Tamurlane, at the head of a combined force of Mongols and Turks, defeated and captured Sultan Bayazid, and in the same year Stefan was able to obtain recognition as despot of Serbia from the Byzantine emperor.

The survival of an independent Serbian state was becoming a real possibility. Unfortunately, Serbian independence was possible only on two conditions: agreement among the Serb leaders and support (or at least benevolent non-aggression) from the Western powers. Neither condition was fulfilled. Hungary and Venice attacked Serbian lands with the hunger and ferocity of starving wolves, and among the Serbs themselves, there was only dissension.

The Serbian Legacy

The Serbian state, which guttered out like an expiring candle in the 15th century, had lasted less than three centuries, and even if we include the developing kingdoms of Raška and Zeta, the history of the Serbs as an independent nation takes in at best five or six centuries. Medieval Serbia left behind no great books, and its feuding rulers can scarcely be said to have provided models for future statesmen. The greatest Serbian king had greatly overextended his empire and at his death left his people in confusion; the noblest Serb leader had died in defeat and failure. Prince Lazar's legacy was not to be a kingdom of this earth, and the Kosovo story, though it may have been created to make defeat and subjugation more bearable, has more than a grain of truth in it, because the soul of medieval Serbia is not revealed either in the ruins of palaces or in the records of military victories.

The Kosovo legacy can only be understood in Kosovo itself, in the monasteries and churches: Gračanica (built by Stefan Milutin in 1310), Visoki Dečani (built by Stefan Dečanski), the Patriarchate of Peć. It is here

Monastery of Morača

and in Mileševa (built by Stefan Vladislav in 1234) and Morača, Žiča (Stefan I), and Studenica (Nemanja), where the Serbian story is told and where the souls of the rulers and the people are truly revealed. Visitors from Western Europe or North America, even those who have spent years prowling through the churches of Italy and France, finds himself in another world, where the Greek East and Latin West not only coexist but fuse into a common Christian idiom.

The meaning of Kosovo was not revealed to only to later generations of Serbs. It grasped immediately by Patriarch Danilo and by Lazar's son, and ever since "the Orthodox Christians of Serbia have captured the entire struggle and deeds of Saint Lazar, the Tsar and Martyr, and the other Martyrs of Kosovo in the brief and inspired words: '*Sve je sveto i čestito bilo, i milome Bogu pristupačno,*' or, 'Everything was holy and honorable, and acceptable to gracious God.'" [5]

The Balšići: Zeta, Again

Lazar and Tvrtko were an exceptional case of harmonious cooperation among Serb dynasts. Closer to home, however, the ruler of Bosnia faced a formidable challenge from Zeta, where the Balšić family was creating an independent powerbase in the latter years of Tsar Uroš's reign. Upon the death of Balša (a fairly obscure local magnate, who may have been one of Dušan's generals)[6] died in 1360, his three sons—Balša, Stratimir, and Djuraj—inherited their father's lands (around Bar and Budva) and began to strengthen their family's network of alliances with the most powerful leaders of Zeta.[7]

To bolster their authority, they also claimed kinship with the Nemanjić dynasty, though they were not above grabbing what they could get from Dušan's crumbling empire.[8] In 1366, the Balšić brothers formally repudiated the sovereign authority of Tsar Uroš "the Weak" and put themselves under the protection of Venice, which gave the Balšići the right to maintain their own fleet in the Adriatic on the condition that their ships were never used to the detriment of the republic's interests—a prudent restriction and a sign that the Venetians did not entirely trust the ambitious brothers.

The Balšić strategy along the coast was to ally themselves with Dubrovnik against Kotor. Their rivals for power in Zeta, the Vojinovići, supported Kotor. In 1367, Nikola Altomanović, who was beginning his failed attempt to make himself the ruler of Serbia, expelled the Vojinovići (who were his nephews) and tried to secure for himself the tribute which Dubrovnik had formerly paid to Uroš. Dubrovnik refused and, with the support of the king of Hungary (the nominal sovereign), forced Altomanović to back down. In 1368, Djuradj and Balša attacked Kotor, but when the Venetians, at King Uroš's request, threatened to intervene, the brothers gave up. In the same year, troubles broke out in the Albanian side of their territory, where the ruler of Durazzo, Karlo Topia, challenged their pretensions. The Balšići later sought an alliance with Topia, to whom they married their sister.[9] Realizing how precarious their relations were with their Catholic subjects in Kotor and Albania, the brothers made a formal submission to Rome in 1369, though there is no evidence that they tried to convert their Orthodox subjects. When Kotor, unimpressed, maintained its loyalty to Emperor Uroš, the Balšići once again attacked the town, only to be stopped again by Venice at Uroš's request.

When Stratimir Balšić died, his brothers divided his lands and established an alliance with King Vukašin. Djuradj married Vukašin's daughter Olivera, and in June 1371, Vukašin and his son Marko arrived in Scutari, at the head of an army, and met with Djuradj. The in-laws agreed to join forces for a campaign against Nikola Altomanović, but the alliance was short-lived. After the death of King Vukašin on the Marica in 1371, Djuradj attacked his brother-in-law, Kraljević ("the prince") Marko and seized Prizren and Peć.

Despite the bad blood between them, Djuradj Balšić then forged a defensive alliance with Nikola Altomanović against Lazar and Tvrtko, who were collaborating closely to put an end to the feudal anarchy that had overtaken Serb lands. Nikola, who had taken refuge with the Balšići, gave his ally lands in Trebinje and Konavle, which lay far from his main territory, and compelled Dubrovnik to pay annual tribute, but Tvrtko and Lazar, anticipating the danger, joined forces and attacked. Capturing Nikola, they blinded the perpetual plotter and divided his lands between them.

The Balšići were successful in putting together a territory greater than Karlo Topia had claimed, but it was a patchwork of Serbs, Albanians, and coastal towns of mixed Slavic-Latin identity, and the crude stitching of the patchwork quickly came undone after Djuradj's death. They lost Prizren (in Kosovo) to Vuk Branković, and in 1379, in the course of a war between Venice and Hungary, the Venetians took Kotor, which, in succeeding years, passed back and forth from Venice to Hungary with depressing regularity.

Djuradj's son was a minor, and his nephew, Balša II, became his successor. Balša married Komita, an heiress of the powerful Musachi family in Albania, and through the marriage, he acquired additional lands in Albania. He was as ambitious as the other Balšići, and like them he wasted his energies in petty territorial squabbles when he might have been forming an alliance against the Turks.[10] In the course of a long war, Balša defeated King Tvrtko of Bosnia, and, breaking with Topia, he added Durazzo to his territory.

The Balšići, to add to their other woes, were divided among themselves. Balša II had completely displaced the son of Djuradj I, and he was quarrelling with his nephew Djuradj II, whom he locked up in Durazzo. Orbini describes Balša as brave but stupid, as well he may have been. In 1385, he led out a small force and attacked a party of Turkish raiders, who defeated Balša, cut off his head, and sent it to the sultan. The Albanian towns were lost to Zeta when they had to be returned to his widow, Komita Musachi, who abandoned her Balšić in-laws to their fate. The Turks succeeded in taking over most of Albania, and the territory held by Balša's nephew and heir Djuradj II was reduced to the region of Lake Skadar and a small portion of the littoral around Ulcinj.

Djuradj II had to fight with the Turks and with his domestic rivals to maintain his possessions. Summoned to a meeting with the Turks (1392), he was taken prisoner and forced to surrender several towns. During his captivity, the Radič Crnojević, whose family was establishing a power base on Lake Scutari, stepped up the campaign to take over Zeta. They quickly seized Budva, and in 1396 they wrested control of Grbalj away from Kotor. Venice also moved in rapidly to grab as much of Djuradj's possessions as they could. While his wife and son were hard-pressed on all sides, Djuradj bargained away part of his remaining territory in order to secure his freedom, but after his release, he sought protection from Venice and Serbia. In 1396, he seized Scutari and Drivast and offered them to his Venetian allies, receiving in return a generous pension for himself and his descendants.

Ten years earlier, in 1386, Djuradj Balšić had cemented relations with Serbia by marrying Knez Lazar's daughter, though it is unlikely that he joined his father-in-law on Kosovo Polje in 1389, a time when he seems to have been collaborating with the Turks. Djuradj apparently preferred to avoid Balkan conflicts and orient himself toward Venice and the Adriatic. This shortsighted policy has been pursued more than once in Montenegro, and it has never worked. Djuradj transferred his capital from Scutari to Ulcinj, where he died about 1403, thoroughly disillusioned with his Venetian ally.

Duradj II's heir, Balša III (1403-1421), was only 17 years old when his father died. His mother, the daughter of Prince Lazar, had disapproved of her husband's pro-Venetian policy and wanted to reorient Zeta toward the Serbs. Venice had not only damaged the economy of the coastal towns by monopolizing trade but also made life difficult for the Orthodox. When Djuradj II's former subjects in Scutari rose up against the harshness of Venetian rule, his mother, Jelena (who managed her young son's affairs), made an attempt to recover some of the family's ancestral lands, and in a conflict with Venice, mother and son turned for help to the Turks. In 1404, young Balša, more myopic even than his father had been, declared himself the sultan's vassal and soon received Turkish military assistance.

Jelena Lazarević was a remarkable woman, capable of maintaining Balšić authority in very difficult times while preserving some of the cultural legacy of the Nemanjić kingdom. Her correspondence (on a variety of intellectual and everyday topics) has been praised for its clarity and sprightliness, and her devotion to the Church is revealed in the number of churches she founded, such as the Mother of God Krajinska, the Church of St Djordje in Beška, and small churches in the islands of Starčeva Gorica and Moranta in Lake Scutari. Most of the churches that used to dot the islands and shoreline of Lake Scutari lie in ruins today, a mute and melancholy witness to the persecution inflicted upon the Orthodox, first by their Turkish and then by their communist overlords. The lake is now only a sapphire gem sparking between the gaunt and barren hills that have been deforested and overgrazed, but while it will take centuries to restore the devastation inflicted by Turks, Venetians, Albanians, and Marxists upon Montenegrin land, the Orthodox Church is already at work, restoring its inheritance, monastery by monastery and church by church.

Fifteenth century Zeta was no place for a weak or irresolute ruler, and those who did not expand their power would probably lose what they inherited. Balša, who was as determined as his forebears to increase his territory, first attacked Kotor, and then, taking advantage of the 1405 rebellion against Venice in Scutari and the surrounding region, he conquered Scutari (briefly and perhaps only the lower town) and Drivast with the assistance of his Turkish allies. Venice struck back, offering a reward to anyone delivering Balša and his mother—dead or alive. Jelena and her son then turned to the Turks for support, but Venice countered by offering the Turks an annual subsidy as "rent" for lands in Zeta.

The advantage passed back and forth between Balša and Venice, each side appealing to the Turks for support. Venice upped the reward money on Balša to 8,000 ducats and promised Ulcinj, Bar, and Budva (as well as 4,000 ducats) to Stefan Crnojević if he could deliver Balsa as a corpse. Sandalj Hranić, a powerful nobleman in Bosnia, agreed to support Venice on condition of receiving Budva as a reward. Hranić had already made himself lord of Kotor and had accepted the submission of the Paštrović clan that inhabited the hills just above the coast. Hranić, who was involved in the salt trade with Italy, challenged Dubrovnik's monopoly of that commerce. Sandalj Hranić was Balša's most serious local rival, but when Balša's mother married Hranić in December 1410, the rival became a powerful ally.

The fortunes of war passed back and forth, and each side signed treaties only to violate the terms. Doge Pietro Loredano of Venice, now in alliance with the Turks, eventually retrieved Ulcinj, Bar, and Budva, as well as a large part of the surrounding area of Scutari and Drivast, and an exhausted and ailing Balša III, pressed and threatened from all sides, fled to his uncle, Despot Stefan Lazarević (Lazar's son), whom he made his heir, dying shortly thereafter. Ultimately, Balša's decision to change partners and embrace the Turks as an ally against Venice only resulted in long and exhausting wars with the Most Serene Republic—to the ultimate benefit of the Turks.

In Balša's absence, the Venetians seized Bar and Ulcinj and seemed in a position to take over the entire coast. However, Despot Stefan, who had formally annexed Zeta to his despotate, entered upon the scene and began to reoccupy one after another of the cities on the coast that had been taken by Venice. Fearing Turkey as a major threat, Despot Stefan hastened to come to terms with his neighbors in Zeta and soon after invested his nephew and future successor, Djuradj Branković, with the governance of Zeta and, to put pressure on Venice, closed the Bojana River to her shipping. Djuradj fought with the Venetians for some time before concluding a peace treaty (in 1423) that recognized, *de facto*, a division of the Serbian and Venetian spheres of interest. In that same year, the Paštrovići, at their annual assembly, pledged their loyalty to Venice, promising tribute and military service. In return, the republic promised to respect the clan's institutions, including its right to select its own vojvoda at the annual assembly. Since previous rulers of Zeta had sent in officials to preside over local affairs, this election was a recent innovation and an indication that the Montenegrin clans were taking advantage of the disorders to increase their autonomy.[11]

Upon the death of Despot Stefan, Djuradj Branković succeeded to the despotate (his title was formally confirmed by the emperor in 1429) and left Zeta. In the power vacuum, Djuradj Djurašević (a member of the Crnojevići) increased his authority while remaining loyal to the despot. Zeta remained somewhat quiet until 1439, when the Turks seized Smederevo, which Djuradj had turned into the thriving economic center of his dwindling despotate. Despairing of assistance from Hungary, he asked the Venetians to give him Ulcinj or, failing that, to grant him permission to pass through their territory with his army or even to settle in Venetian land. They refused Ulcinj but did allow him to pass through their territory. Along the way, Djuradj was hailed by the inhabitants of Istria and Dalmatia, and he returned to Bar, where he attempted, with Venetian help, to make peace with Turkey.

Realizing the futility of his efforts, he withdrew to Dubrovnik and ordered his subjects to put themselves under the protection of Venice. Dubrovnik welcomed Djuradj and turned a deaf ear to Sultan Murad II's blandishments—he offered the territory, freedom from tribute, and the right of free trade throughout the Ottoman Empire. In gratitude, the despot deposited his considerable treasure with Dubrovnik, and in 1441 he went by way of Dalmatia to Hungary.

Upon Djuradj's departure, Stefan Vukčić Kosača, Sandalj's successor in Hum, seized Trebinje and entered Zeta. This was all the provocation that Venice needed to take over the former Balšić lands on the pretext that they were foiling a usurpation and fulfilling their agreement with Despot Djuradj. In response, Stefan Vukčić Hum, acting in concert with his rival Stefan Crnojević (son of Djuradj Djurašević), conquered Bar, and only the arrival of winter prevented them from attacking Skadar. The Venetians were unwilling to relinquish the struggle, and they not only they retook most of the towns they had lost but won over Stefan Crnojević to their side. By this time, however, Djuradj Branković, with Hungarian help, had restored the despotate and renewed his claims on Zeta. The Venetians refused to give up territory on which they had spent so much of their resources, but they cut a deal with Djuradj in the hope of using him in the campaign to eliminate George Castriotis "Skenderbeg," the Serbian-Albanian hero who was attempting to resist the Turks.

In 1454, there was turmoil throughout the Balkans[13], and all hopes were dashed for a Serbian state when the Turks captured Novo Brdo and divided up the despotate. About this time Stefan Vukčić assumed the title "Herceg of Saint Sava" (a title later confirmed by the Holy Roman emperor), and the lands he governed came to be known as Hercegovina.

Crnojevići

In the struggles for succession after the Balšić family, Stefan (or Stefanica) Crnojević rapidly emerged as the leading contender for power, and during the period leading up to the fall of the Serbian Despotate, he succeeded in making himself the most powerful feudal lord in Zeta. When the Turks seized the despotate, the Crnojević family was in a position to make itself the last dynasty of Zeta and the first of Crna Gora, which was the name the Crnojević family used for their lands, which lay in the mountains north of Lake Scutari.[14] (The name is probably even older, used by the Paštrovići to designate the mountains rising up from the coast.)

Continuing the Balšić policy of seeking alliances in Albania, Stefan married the sister of George Castriotis, the Serb-Albanian hero of Albanian resistance against the Turks. Stefan's son Djuradj was later married to the daughter of Karlo Musachi Topia, the heir of two powerful Albanian families. In 1447, Castriotis attacked and plundered the coast around Ulcinj and Bar, and in June of the following year, the despot marched to Kotor Bay to reassume his authority. The Paštrovići, whose leaders were pledged to Venice, rose up against Venetian Kotor and supported the despot.

The Venetians, looking for an ally, wooed Stefan Crnojević, who realized the advantage to be gained from distancing himself from the central authority of Despot Djuradj. In 1452, he acknowledged the suzerainty of Venice, which recognized Stefan as "supreme vojvoda of Zeta" and granted him a stipend of 500 ducats *per annum*. The agreement created dissensions in the Crnojević family, but Stefanica emerged as the winner. The agreement with Venice naturally strained relations between the despot and Crnojević. The Venetians, for their part, had become serious about converting the region to Catholicism, and they began systematically expelling Orthodox priests from their churches.

When the Grbljani clan (a brave people living up the coast from Budva) rose against Venice and Kotor, Stefan put down the rebellion with considerable brutality. The despot's forces, however, seized Žabljak (on Lake Scutari) only to lose it in a counterattack. In the end, Stefan Crnojević was able to expand his lands to the River Morača and territory on both sides of the Zeta and Morača Rivers as well as the area around Podgorica.

When the Turks took Medun in 1456, Crnojević was forced to repulse Turkish attacks and form a closer relationship with Venice. In 1455, he had concluded a treaty with Venice in which he recognized Venetian suzerainty in exchange for a pledge from the republic to respect Montenegrin laws and not to interfere in her economy. In addition to Venice and the Despot Djuradj Branković, who were both bidding for Stefan Crnojević's support, Stefan Vukčić Kosača was also becoming increasingly involved in the affairs of Zeta. Crnojević finally opted for Stefan Vukčić Kosača, giving his son Ivan as hostage, who stayed with Stefan Vukčić for ten years.

Stefan was succeeded by his son Ivan Crnojević (1465-1490), who tried to rid himself of Venetian influence. After stirring up the Grbljani and the Paštrović clan, Ivan launched an attack on Kotor but failed to take it. Subsequently, Ivan and Venice reconciled and restored the cooperative agreement set up by Stefan. Ivan was required to join the Venetians in their struggles in Albania, which caused renewed problems with Turkey.

In order to put an end to the frequent Turkish raids, Ivan recognized Turkish suzerainty in 1471 (without repudiating Venice) and was under an obligation to pay 700 ducats annual tribute. As Ivan remained loyal to Venice, the Turks continued to raid his territory. Ivan stopped paying tribute after losing lands on the left banks of the Morača and Zeta Rivers. Venice conferred upon him an aristocratic title and promised him military aid and a refuge if he were defeated by the Turks. After the battle of Scutari, in which Ivan triumphed, he was able to follow up his victory while Turkey was distracted in Asia Minor. Ivan erected a chain of fortresses, of which the best known is in Obod. Together with Vojvoda Vlatko Vuković of Hercegovina, whose lands the Turks had demanded, he waged wars against Turkey with initial success. Vlatko's brother Stefan, however, converted to Islam, joined the Turks in attacking Ivan, and began to work on his brother to join him. This was an ominous development that presaged much mischief.

In early 1477, the Turks launched fresh conquests. One Turkish army attacked Albania and another, Upper Zeta. In 1478, the Crnojević capital Žabljak (on Lake Scutari) fell. Ivan sought shelter in Italy, and Montenegro fell under Turkish dominion temporarily. As the Turks were preoccupied with internal strife in the empire after the death of Sultan Mehmed II (1481), Ivan returned to the country and came to terms with Sultan Bayazid II.

Realizing that he could not defend Žabljak, Ivan burned the town and, in 1475, made Obod the capital of the Crnojević state. Soon after he moved his headquarters to Cetinje, an obscure settlement under Mt. Lovćen, used by surrounding tribes only for summer grazing. The area came to be known as Katunska Nahija ("Hut County") because of the shepherds' huts (*katuni*) that dotted the entire highland valley. There, in 1482, he established his own official residence, and two years later, in fulfillment of a vow he had made in Italy, he erected the monastery of Cetinje, dedicated to the Mother of God, and made it the seat of the metropolitanate of Zeta.

Failing to find assistance from Italy, Ivan was determined to preserve the core of a Serbian state within the inaccessible mountains of Montenegro. He knew he would have to rely on the bravery and sturdy independence of the Montenegrin people. He also restricted trade with coastal towns and stimulated the development of handicrafts, hoping to make his state economically independent.

Ivan granted a large number of privileges to tribal chiefs, who gained the independence they would need to carry on the struggle against the Turks. Gathered in a public assembly, his people swore never to abandon the struggle against the Turks. They promised to dishonor any man who gave up the fight, give him an apron and a spindle, and set the women, brandishing their own spindles, to chase him as a coward and traitor.

In order to develop more peaceful relations with Venice, Ivan married his son Djuradj to the daughter of a Venetian nobleman—a move that was not welcomed in Montenegro. Ivan died while his son was in Italy, passing into legend as a hero who would some day return to defend the Serbs from the Muslim Turks, whom he would drive from Europe. Upon his return from Italy, Djuradj Crnojević assumed power in 1490. Although he was not successful in meeting increased pressure from both Turks and Venetians, Djuradj did promote the cultural advancement of his people. He founded a printing press in which the first Serbian book in Cyrillic was printed (in 1493).

Toward the end of his reign, Djuradj attempted to secure help from the Kingdom of Naples with the aim of stirring up Albanian tribes in Southern Italy and creating unrest in Turkey. Djuradj's brother Stefan, however, had made an arrangement with the Turks, who agreed to recognize him as ruler of Zeta if he converted to Islam. Djuradj was forced to leave the country and to seek help from Venice, telling his people to respect the metropolitan as the ruler of the country in his absence. Although the Venetians initially granted him both a refuge and a pittance to live on, they later imprisoned Djuradj in order to ingratiate themselves with the sultan, whom the exiled vojvoda was "slandering."

Stefan was the nominal ruler of Montenegro for two years until he was forced to leave, and Montenegro fell under direct Turkish rule. During this period, the renegade may sought refuge in the Albanian village of Bušatlija, because it was believed in later years that the hereditary viziers of Scutari, the Bušatlji, were descended from Stefan Crnojević. Djuradj, in the meantime, wanted to return from Venice and recover his throne, and he entered into negotiations with the sanjak-bey of Skadar, who sent him to Istanbul, where he is said to have converted to Islam and lived for a while off of an estate the sultan granted him in Anatolia. He is also said to have made his escape and returned to Italy, but little can be said for certain of his career after he left Montenegro.

Djuradj's departure to Turkey closed the final chapter of Montenegrin independence. In 1497, the Turks did allow a cousin of Stefan to succeed, at least in name, and in the same year Venice relinquished her protectorate. The territory was eventually put under the control of Djuradj's renegade younger brother, who took the name Staniša Skenderbeg and ruled Zeta from Scutari (from which the region became known as Skaderia).

The Serbs' century-long failure to unite against the Turks, coupled with the shortsighted and predatory strategy of Venice and Hungary, had long-lasting repercussions in the Balkans: slavery, oppression, and cultural genocide—the legacy of Islamic rule in Europe. The survival of the Serbian nation must have seemed a doubtful proposition, though between the end of the 15th century, when Montenegro fell under Turkish domination, and the beginning of the 19th century, when the wars of liberation broke out, there was hardly a generation of Serbs that did not rise up in rebellion against the Turks. In Montenegro, as in other Serb lands, the national myth was nourished on the tales and songs of the Kosovo heroes, Prince Lazar and Milos Obilić (who killed the sultan in his tent). To expel the Turks from Serbia and take revenge for Kosovo was the duty of every Serb, and the Montenegrins, throughout the cold dark years of misery and oppression, warmed themselves by the fire lit in the Serbian imagination by the Kosovo story.

Notes

The best scholarly source for medieval Serbia in English, apart from works on Byzantine history, are Fine's two volumes on the medieval Balkans. Sima Ćirković provides a coherent and straightforward account of the period. Temperly's history is still worth reading, and there is a fund of surprisingly good information (though not on Zeta) in the second volume of the Prince and Princess Lazarovich-Hreblianovich's *The Servian People*.

1. Fine II, pp. 2-3. It is also argued that the brothers are descended from Desa, brother of Uroš II.

2. Fine II, pp. 43.

3. Gopčević, pp. 34-35.

4. On Serbian ethnicity, see Vlahović.

5. Popovich in Velimirović and Popovich, p. 39.

6. Miklošič, *Monumenta Serbica*, pp. 141-3.

7. *Istorija naroda Jugoslavije* I, p. 451.

8. On the testimony of Mauro Orbini, p. 286; cf. *Istorija srpskog naroda*, II, p.27.

9. The records are very confusing, but Gopčević, pp. 49-50 makes some sense of them.

10. See Soulis, pp. 139ff.

12. Fine, p. 517.

13. Phrantzes xxxvii.

14. *Istorija naroda Jugoslavije* I, p. 460.

THE STRUGGLE FOR LIBERATION

They rose to where their sovereign eagle sails,
They kept their faith, their freedom, on the height,
Chaste, frugal, savage, arm'd by day and night
Against the Turk; whose inroad nowhere scales
Their headlong passes, but his footstep fails,
And red with blood the Crescent reels from fight
Before their dauntless hundreds, in prone flight
By thousands down the crags, and thro' the vales.
O smallest among peoples! rough rock-throne
Of Freedom! warriors beating back the swarm
Of Turkish Islam for five hundred years,
Great Tsernagora! Never since thine own
Black ridges drew the cloud and brake the storm
Has breathed a race of mightier mountaineers.

—"Montenegro" by Alfred Lord Tennyson

Serbs cannot always understand the motives of their enemies, to whom they often attribute deep and complex motives for their perfidy. During the 1990's, when so many members of "the best Congress money can buy" were stoutly pro-Albanian and anti-Serb, many Serbs, convinced there had to be a more profound motive than the power of money, came to believe Sen. Robert Dole had an Albanian mother. Montenegrins, 500 years earlier, refused to accept the fact that some members of the Serb nobility were willing to betray their faith and their people for the sake of personal advantage. The betrayal of Staniša (Maksim, as he is sometimes known in the poems) Crnojević was an event recalled with bitterness.

One explanation offered by later poets (in the "The Wedding of Maksim Crnojević") was that his father, Ivan, had arranged a marriage for Maksim and the doge's daughter, who was told of her fiancé's good looks. In Ivan's absence, however, the son had been disfigured by illness, and the family cooked up a scheme to trick the bride. Discovering the fraud—and her husband's ugliness—the proud Venetian girl repudiated the marriage and wanted all the pres-ents back. Humiliated, Maksim tells his father he is going to Constantinople to convert to Islam. (Some day, perhaps, they will be singing of "Skenderbob," the half-Albanian who, cursed by God for his apostasy, lost the use of his arm.)

Such inventions must have been small consolation in the dark days of the 16th century, when Montenegro was being forged, both as a people and as a state. Under attack from the Turks, Serbs retreated with their families into the mountains and stubbornly resisted the Muslim invaders for centuries. These men were warriors who fought to live and who lived to fight, and there was little place, even in a monastery, for gentle souls who cherished a quiet life and the arts of civilization. It has been said of all the victims of Turkish conquest that those who would not be slaves must be savages; and this saying applies to Greeks, Albanians, and Armenians as much as it does to the Serbs.

The Montenegro that emerged through the centuries of resistance to Turkish domination consisted of three regions. The Littoral (*Primorje*) was a narrow coastal strip, sometimes extending into adjacent highlands, that was always under the direct rule or dominating influence of foreigners—first the Roman and Byzantine Empires, then Venice, and finally Austria-Hungary. Montenegro-proper, or "Old Montenegro" (*Stara Crna Gora*), was the land lying north and east of the coastal strip and extending roughly to the River Zeta flowing from Nikšić to Podgorica. On the other side of the Zeta were the Highlands (*Brda*), extending from Old Montenegro to the River Lim.

Although both Old Montenegro and Brda are mountainous areas, the soil and terrain are distinct. Old Montenegro is arid, rocky, and barren, while in Brda we encounter lush highland pastures and well-watered forests. Well into the 19th century, the two regions were regarded as entities distinct from each other and from the communities on the coast. Thus, we read of the people of "Montenegro and Brda" rebelling against the Turks, or of the "Brdjani" collaborating with "Montenegrins." In the 19th century, the boundaries of the Principality of Montenegro were pushed into Hercegovina, to include "Old Hercegovina" to the west and northwest of Nikšić. Divided as they were, Montenegrins shared a certainly lordly quality that struck one Victorian as proof of their aristocratic lineage: "Put [him] in a drawing-room, and the Montenegrin, who has never bowed his neck to a foreign master, will look and behave like a gentleman."[1]

Organization of the Clans

Montenegro proved to be a hard nut for the Turkish jaw to crack, though the early 16th century gave little reason for hope for the "smallest among peoples." The ruling Crnojevići (and too many other Montenegrin leaders) had converted to Islam and made submission to the sultan, and land-hungry Turkish colonists were swarming over the country, establishing their settlements as so many outposts for the expansion of both Islamic religion and Turkish authority. It was in this difficult period that the Serbian peoples of the mountains slowly reorganized their life into the system of clan (*pleme*) and brotherhood (*bratstvo*) that would become an effective basis on which to build the eventual counterattack.

Like the Greeks and Romans, and the Celts and Germans in their early days, the Slavic nations were organized by families and extended kingroups. These were not, as it has been frequently alleged, expressions of primitive tribal communism, but (as Aristotle recognized in the *Politics*) the natural basis of human social organization.[2] Even Athens, during its most creative period, was organized into brotherhoods of kinfolks and "demes," territorial units dominated by a few intermarried extended families. In times of crisis, the Serbian people of Montenegro quite naturally fell back on kinship as the most effective principle of social community, and they creatively reorganized themselves into the loose pyramid of household-brotherhood-clan that became the bastion of their moral and cultural resistance.

Throughout the dark days of persecution and oppression, Montenegrins stubbornly refused to surrender their Christian religion or their Serbian identity, and the story of their heroic resistance is one of the brightest chapters in the history of mankind's too often futile pursuit of freedom. Like the ancient Greeks who learned their history from the heroic stories of the *Iliad* and *Odyssey*, Montenegrins preserved their history by singing the songs, handed down from one generation to another, that celebrated the exploits of god-like heroes, their hard-fought battles, raids and forays, victories won and massacres endured. The development of the clan structure was an evolutionary process, as kin-groups and "brotherhoods" slowly acquired a sense of larger identity. Brotherhoods might develop in a variety of ways, but by tradition the members of a brotherhood could trace ancestry back to a common progenitor. As in Scotland, the clans were based both on kinship and on geography: Each clan was responsible for defending its own territory. The territories of the clans corresponded to the territories of the districts, and the number of districts in the late 17th century corresponded to the number of clans in the 19th century.

Brotherhoods consisted of families, which were, in turn, made up of households. There was no "tribal communism" in Montenegro. Although the clans held pasturelands in common, the households possessed their own property and looked after their own needs. Though each family had a *glava* (head), who was certainly more than *primus inter pares*, each member of a household and family was something like a citizen who had the same rights as other members. This principle of family democracy existed also on the level of clans. Important decisions were made by an assembly that could be attended by any member of a clan, while executive authority was vested in the council of tribal headmen, made up of the chieftain, the headmen of the fraternities, and, occasionally, other distinguished married men. The most influential of the headmen came from the strongest brotherhoods within the clan. At the head of stood the chieftain (*vojvoda*) who served as military leader.

In their unending conflict with the clans, local Turkish authorities sought leverage by setting one clan against another. In 1634, for instance, the Turks made use of clan animosities when they suppressed a rebellion of the Kuč and Piper clans, which broke out when they refused to pay tribute. The Montenegrin clans were as quarrelsome as their counterparts in Scotland and Ireland, and highland Montenegro was disturbed by blood feuds and wars over pastures and water rights. Raiding caravans and attacking rival settlements became an honorable way of life, as it was on the Scottish-English border. The bold cattle-raider or highwayman was not condemned as a criminal but celebrated in song as a hero in the fight for freedom. It was regular work (lowland farming in particular) that was beneath a warrior's dignity. To die in bed of old age was something ignoble, an attitude summed up in the phrase, *usmrtio se*—a sort of portmanteau word combining the meanings, "he died—he stank."

Although the clans were generally a law unto themselves, institutions that expressed national unity did evolve, including a Montenegrin assembly, in which the bishop and the chieftains cast their votes, and a people's court, which had 24 jurors (headmen). Typically, however, Montenegrin political allegiance in those days was exercised at the clan level, and the clan chieftains acknowledged no higher secular authority. The Crnojević brothers had, after all, exhausted their credibility. Djuradj came to regret his abandonment and betrayal of the people: Within four years of his submission to the sultan, he disappeared from Turkey and showed up in Venice seeking the republic's assistance in recovering his country. The Venetians, however, were not interested in helping a ruler who had proved himself so unreliable, much less in aggravating relations with the Turks. Instead of helping Djuradj, Venice preferred to seize parts of his lands along the coast, including Soli and Grbalj, whose salt works were a valuable asset. Trade in salt was a primary source of Venetian revenue in the Littoral during this period.[3]

The Turkish Order

The apostasy of Staniša Crnojević had grave consequences for the future of Montenegro. The renegade Montenegrins who had followed Staniša's lead were allowed to remain and practice their new faith in their old country, even where Skenderbey was unable to exert his authority. Ready at all times to join hands with the Turkish invaders, these Muslims became a constant source of danger. This pattern of betrayal and collaboration led finally to the terrible "Montenegrin Vespers" in the reign of Danilo I.

In the war between Venice and Turkey (1499-1503), the main theatre was in the Peloponnese, but Montenegro was also the scene of some fighting, in which plague may have claimed more victims than combat. In the end, the Turks annexed the region that had been ruled by Djuradj Crnojević to the territory of the *sanjak-bey* (governor) of Scutari, who ruled the region thorough his *subashi* (military district commander) headquartered in Žabljak (the fortified town near Podgorica, as opposed to the Žabljak on Mt. Durmitor). This sanjak-bey was none other than Staniša—now known as "Skenderbey" (not to be confused with the better known Albanian leader with the same name). The Turks also maintained military outposts in Podgorica and Medun, from which they were able to control the valleys as well as the Highlands. Montenegro fell under the jurisdiction of a *kadi*, a judge who administered Islamic law, and divided into seven *nahije* (counties). In 1513, it became a separate *sanjak* (district) under Skender-bey's administration.

In large parts of Montenegro, Turkish administration was largely theoretical at first, and Stefan Crnojević and his cousin the sanjak-bey nevertheless appear to have lived for a time on reasonable terms. On Stefan's death in 1515, the Turks did not oppose the succession of his son Ivan, who a few months later made way for his son Djuradj. This prince, the last of the Crnojević rulers of Montenegro, remained barely a year in his rough domain, however. The son of one Venetian lady and the husband of another, himself a patrician of the Serenissima and its long-time resident, he had the utmost distaste for a life of solitude and privation in Cetinje. His wife joined her complaints to his own, and Djuradj decided to leave Montenegro forever. He summoned the chiefs and people, told them his intentions, and entrusted them with the weapons that his great ancestors Stefan and Ivan the Black had wielded in defense of their liberties. To the Bishop Vavilo (Babylas), as the next most important personage to himself, he confided the task of governing the country. So it happened that an ecclesiastic, who combined the functions of priest, lawyer, and leader in war, ruled Montenegro.

The builders of empire are always in search of cheap labor in the forms of slaves, serfs or sweatshop workers, and taxpayers. Throughout the Balkans, the victorious Turks seized the land and reduced the farmers to the level of serfs and sharecroppers. Whatever they could not steal, they taxed. The collection of taxes was a constant preoccupation of the rulers of occupied Montenegro. In his own lifetime, the Prophet of Islam established the model for subsequent relations between Muslim conquerors and their Christian subjects: "Fight those who do not profess the true faith (Islam) till they pay the *jiziya* (poll tax) with the hand of humility." Nine hundred years later, Islam's advance proceeded in the Balkans along the same lines. The option of conversion was always available to its surviving victims, but the collection of taxes from the Christian remnant was both the symbolic key to their submission and a religious duty of the

Cetinje

Turk. The vanquished populations were "protected," at least in theory, provided they submitted to the Muslim rulers' conditions, but in Montenegro, at least, "protection" was extended to the conquered non-Muslims on the condition that they agreed to a "pact" (*Dhimma*) that imposed degrading and discriminatory regulations.

On that basis, much of the Ottoman experience was in ruling over developed countries that had cities, a commercial life, and agricultural estates on which cash crops were raised. Taxation, under such circumstances, was a comparatively straightforward affair. In much of Montenegro, however, people lived on a subsistence level, neither owning assets nor earning money that could be profitably taxed. Ottoman officials were aware of the region's poverty and understood the impossibility of maintaining an elaborate bureaucratic apparatus. In 1523, a special law thus described Montenegro as an "impassable mountainous country, and the *raya* (the 'horde' of non Turkish subjects) cannot pay the tithe, poll tax, tribute and other dues."

Accommodating themselves to "heathen customs," Turkish rulers introduced lump-sum taxation and made each household (there were over 3,000) and estate theoretically subject to a tax of 55 silver pieces: three to the sultan, 20 to the sanjak-bey, and two to the tax collector. Subject households were also responsible for supplying an annual 15 days of labor in the salt works in Grbalj. Converts to Islam were exempt from these exactions, but their chieftains were responsible for collecting the taxes as the only intermediaries between the Turkish authorities and the heads of families. Many of the conflicts with the Turks began as tax protests, and over the years Montenegrins learned that the life of a *hajduk* (outlaw) had its advantages.

In the second half of the 16th century, the number of Muslims in Montenegro was on the increase, particularly in the more fertile areas and in the towns. Muslims seized estates and fisheries for themselves and did not refrain from putting their hands on monastic lands, which they either confiscated directly or burdened with tithes. Their high-handed confiscations were not always authorized by the Turkish central authority, but they were almost invariably tolerated. Most of the time, the Montenegrins' chief problems did not lie so much with the sultan or the officials of the Ottoman Empire directly responsible to the central authority as with the local Muslim landlords, who were well aware of their Christian origins and uncomfortable with the memory. Their recently acquired identity prompted them to view the Orthodox population more as prey than as imperial subjects. The only obstacle to their tyrannical abuse of power was presented by the autonomy of the Montenegrin clans themselves.

The lot of the raya became more unbearable after the Turkish debacle at Vienna in 1683, which put an end to Turkish plans to expand the empire farther into Europe. It was a difference in degree rather than kind, however: The oppression of Christians in the Balkans began when Turks occupied a region, and it did not end until they were expelled.

Divide and Rule

As early as 1520, the newly established Turkish authority under Skenderbey Crnojević had to send a military expedition to deal with Montenegrin restlessness. In subsequent decades, the Ottomans' vast empire, inefficient administrative structure, and overcommitted military gave frequent opportunities for Montenegrin uprisings, even at a time when the power of the Turk was at its height. Montenegro's refusal to submit was reflected in the readiness of its people to join any enemy of Turkey, as soon as its sails appeared on the horizon.

An early instance came in 1537, when a combined Venetian-Spanish fleet entered Kotor Bay and proceeded to take Kotor and Herceg-Novi, where the Spanish established a garrison. With the help of Hercegovinian Serbs they successfully defended their position until in 1539 a massive Turkish force—of reportedly 90,000 men—besieged and bombarded the city with 13,000 shells for 25 days. The garrison of 4,000 men at the beginning of the campaign was slowly whittled down to a fraction of its former strength, but it held out. The Turks were on the verge of lifting their siege when two Spanish deserters revealed how few men were left inside. The news prompted renewed attacks. When the Spanish eventually surrendered, the Hercegovinian duke killed his wife and two daughters to prevent their forcible conversion to Islam and the humiliation always inflicted upon captive Christian women. When he was subsequently captured the Turks at first offered to spare him if he converted; and upon his refusal, they tortured and impaled the recalcitrant duke. A treaty was signed in 1543, dividing the Montenegrin coastline between Turkey and Venice, though the conflict was renewed in the 1570's.

The struggle between Venice and the Turks over Montenegro was played out against the larger conflict between the Islamic and Christian worlds. In the great Christian naval victory at Lepanto (on the Gulf of

Patras in the Peloponnese), Jevrem Bizanti, an admiral in Kotor's "Seaman's Brotherhood," fought heroically before going down with his ship.

European rulers must have viewed Montenegro in this period—and until much later—as a no-man's land. In the early 17th century, a plot was hatched between the Pope and Spain to reconquer much of the eastern Mediterranean from the Turks and to give Albania (a loose term that was used to designate much of the western Balkans, including Montenegro) and Macedonia to the Duke of Savoy, who claimed descent from the Byzantine imperial family, the Palaeologoi. The plans got far enough that in 1608, the Serbian Patriarch promised to crown the duke as king. At virtually the same time, agents for the duke of Nevers (a claimant to the dukedom of Mantova) stirred up the people of Majina, in the hills above Budva, to revolt against Turkish taxation. The chief plotter was Père Joseph, later famous as Richelieu's confessor, who in 1619 proclaimed a new crusade against the infidels, but the Duke of Nevers, after making good his claim to Mantova, lost all interest in Montenegro.[4]

Bishops Rule

The Turks had more than Venetians or French priests to deal with in the 16th century. Conflicts inevitably arose between the Turkish feudal landowners and the native Christian leaders of the clans, and in this contest Venice was neither willing nor able to help. Fragmented into feuding clans, Montenegro lacked the political unity that could concentrate the scattered resistance into a comprehensive movement for liberation. The one visible embodiment of the Serbian-Montenegrin identity was the Orthodox Church, which maintained the sense of territorial and cultural integrity and preserved the memory of the Serbian state and the Nemanjić era. After the last Crnojević left for Venice, Bishop Vavilo in Cetinje effectively had control of whatever civil jurisdiction remained in Old Montenegro for some 20 years.

The institution of the Vladika (bishop-prince) saved Montenegro from the fate of Serbia and Bosnia, where discord among the vying princelings paved the way for the Turk. Unlike the secular rulers, whose apostasy was bitterly remembered, a monk was not likely to seek personal advantage by renouncing his religion. For 180 years after their first appointment, the Vladikas were elected by the chiefs and people. During the greater part of this period the history of the country consisted of little more than one continuous struggle for existence against the Turks, amid which it is difficult to distinguish the shadowy figures of the successive prelates.

The history of the Serbian Orthodox Church in Montenegro is long and varied. Until the autocephalous Serbian Church was established by Saint Sava, the muddled pattern of jurisdictions within the Balkans reflected the see-saw between Rome and Constantinople as well as the various efforts, by Serbs and Bulgars, to establish national churches. The picture cleared up, however, after 1219, when the Ecumenical Patriarch granted the Serbian Church autocephaly, a grant confirmed by Emperor Theodore Laskaris. Sava divided the church into nine or ten dioceses, one of which was Zeta, in the southern part of Montenegro. For the first bishop, Sava selected his own disciple, Ilarion, whose seat was the Monastery of St. Michael in Prevlaka, near Tivat. At a church council in Skoplje presided over by Stefan Dušan, the diocese of Zeta was elevated to a metropolitanate. When the Venetians invaded the littoral, destroyed St. Michael's, and began persecuting the Orthodox clergy, the bishop's seat was moved successively to Budva, to Bar, to Vranjina on Lake Scutari, to St. Nicholas' Monastery in Obod (Rijeka Crnojevića), and finally to Cetinje Monastery, which was constructed in 1484.

In the meantime, the Turks had abolished the Serbian patriarchate, but the Grand Vizier Mehmed-pasha Sokolović—a Bosnian Serb by birth—was mindful of his suffering people from whom he had been snatched as a child, and he restored the Patriarchate in 1557, making his brother the Patriarch. After 1557, the Serbian patriarch in Peć consecrated Montenegrin bishops, once they had been chosen by the synod of priests. However, in 1766 the Turks, fearful of the rising spirit of Serb patriotism, again abolished the patriarchate and put the Serbian Orthodox Church under the control of Greek "Phanariot" bishops, who were often concerned more with subordinating the Serbs to the Greek hierarchy—and lining their own pockets—than with providing for their spiritual needs.

As unwilling to submit to Greek bishops as they were to pay taxes to the sanjak-bey, Montenegrins had to find other authorities who could consecrate the *vladika*—a term that designates bishops as well as rulers (*despotes* in Greek is the nearest equivalent). First, they turned to the Serbian metropolitans residing in Sremski Karlovci (German Karlowitz) in Austria, just north of Belgrade, and later to the Russians. If the Montenegrin bishops were "independent" in this sense from the rest of the Serbian Church, it was from necessity and not from choice. It was not until after World War I that the Montenegrin bishops voted unanimously to place the metropolitanate under the jurisdiction of the reestablished Serbian Patriarchate.

While the influence of the Monastery of Morača, founded by the Nemanjići in the 14th century, was strong in Brda, in Old Montenegro the Church was centered in the Cetinje Monastery, where the metropolitans were becoming the social as well as the spiritual leaders of the people. Fragmented into clans, Montenegrin Serbs eventually turned to their Vladikas as the only leaders capable of representing the nation. The progress of this true love between the bishops and their people was not always smooth. As late as 1638, peasants in the area around Cetinje usurped some Church lands, and, according to Bishop Mardarije, "started stealing from the Monastery, leaving it hungry and thirsty." But even those wild clansmen eventually realized that the Church was the only tangible remnant of the glory that once was the Nemanjić Kingdom.

Monastery of Cetinje

Between Venice and Turkey

Montenegro enjoyed comparative peace in the 16th century. Bishop Vavilo was allowed to preside over his restive clans and to devote his attention to the printing press at Obod, which issued books of devotion bearing his name on the titlepage. Some of them are still extant. Under his successor, Bishop German, one of the Crnojević Muslims (Petar) tried to enforce his hereditary claim, only to be driven out of the lands he claimed.

The Turks were too much occupied with the Hungarian war to take revenge, and it was not till 1570 that Montenegro had to face an Ottoman invasion when the sanjakbey of Scutari Ali Pasha revived the claims of Staniša to the Montenegrin throne. The converts to Islam welcomed the Pasha's troops with open arms. With their help, he was able to seize the fortress of Obod and destroy the precious printing press. The Montenegrins were forced to pay the harach, or tribute, even though it merely "defrayed the cost of the Sultan's slippers."

The shame of that memory could not be eradicated, and the Montenegrins' refusal to pay tribute was the cause of a new Turkish invasion in 1604, during the reign of Bishop Rufin. A Turkish force of 3,000 crossed the Morača and burnt villages until they were caught in a Montenegrin ambush in which many of the invaders were killed. This victory encouraged Montenegrin hajduks to send out ever more ambitious raiding parties that reached across southern Serbia and as far as Bulgaria.

In 1612, the exasperated Sultan sent a larger force to bring the bandits to heel and pacify the area with an army reliably estimated at 25,000. Their mission was foiled, however, when the Montenegrins withdraw into remote mountain areas. The Turks followed, burning villages along the way, but when the Montenegrins swooped down in a counterattack just north of Podgorica, the Turks retreated in disarray. The uselessness of their cavalry in the gorges decided the day. A year later, a still larger Turkish invasion force was assembled by Arslan Pasha; the invaders were said to have been twice as numerous as the total number of souls in Montenegro. But the mountaineers again knew how to make use of the terrain. After six months of skirmishing, they swooped down from their redoubts and routed the attackers.

After another unsuccessful attempt at forcing Montenegro to submit, by Suleiman Pasha of Scutari in 1623, Montenegro enjoyed over 60 years of relative peace—until Venice prompted Montenegro to join the campaign against the Turks in 1687. In the course of the 17th century, Venice played an ever-larger role in Montenegrin political life, initially in the coastal areas but eventually throughout the country.

An early description of the conditions in Montenegro came from a patrician from Venice, Mariano Bolizza, whose detailed account (published in 1614) told of the Montenegrins' unparalleled valor and military prowess. The doges took note and sought help from the mountaineers in their own disputes with Turkey. Early in the Candian war between Turkey and the Republic of Venice in 1646-47, the Paštrovići living in the hills above Budva and the Pobori clan and the Grbljani took the Venetian side. But this was a local affair, unlike the events of 1687, when the Serbs of Montenegro and Hercegovina, instigated by Venice, rose up in arms against the Turks and expelled them from many of their strongholds.

These events took place against the wider backdrop of Kara-Mustapha's defeat outside Vienna by the Polish King John Sobieski in 1683 and the rout of the Turks at Mohacs in 1687. The emperor's armies crossed the Sava and the Danube, and many parts of Serbia and Bosnia were in the hands of the Austrians. The imperial cause was aided by an uprising fomented by Djordje Branković, who claimed to be descended from Serbian princes. The fighting was bitter in Montenegro and Hercegovina. In the contest over Grahovo, the Serbs—now for the first time generally equipped with firearms—defended the town, which they had taken previously. The Serbs drove off the Turks, whose commander was lucky to escape with his life. A small Montenegrin force then took Ulcinj from the Turks, and went on to demolish dozens of Turkish outposts.

In 1688, Venice made peace with the sultan. Their real conflicts with the Turks, after all, were in the Peloponnese and in the Aegean; Serbs were expendable. Venice's departure from the scene enabled Suleiman-pasha of Scutari to turn his undivided attention to the republic's abandoned partner. He collected an army of foot and horse and attacked Montenegrins in Brda. A contingent of Venetian soldiers a thousandstrong withdrew at the critical moment, and in vain did Vladika Visarion remind the treacherous republic that it was for her sake that his people had incurred the wrath of the Turk. The bishop died soon afterward, poisoned—according to the Montenegrin chroniclers—by the Venetians. Mistrust of the "Latins" explains the absence of Montenegrins in Venetian service in the following years.

Suleiman-pasha finally took Cetinje in 1692, and the fleeing monks had to bury their relics and the great bell, which has never been discovered. Gunpowder had been stockpiled in the monastery, and as the Turkish soldiers were entering the building, the monks set off the powder, killing hundreds of Turks but also destroying the monastery. Many precious books and manuscripts were also lost, and the revered building remained in ruins for many years. During a few years of respite offered by the Turks, who were at war on the lower Danube, Visarion's successor Bishop Sava was able to spend his brief reign restoring the morale of his people as well as reconstructing the buildings that had been destroyed. By the time the Turks were free to attack Montenegro yet again, a new bishop was ready to defend it as it had never been defended before. This was Bishop Danilo, the first Vladika of the Petrović family.

It was about this time, in the early 18th century, that the folk epic "The Piperi and Tahir Pasha" is set. The poem, though it is not an historical record, recounts the defiance of the Piperi clan, when Tahir-pasha of Scutari demands a tribute of money, hostages, and eight beautiful girls who will serve as concubines. The Piperi are shamed into resistance when one young hostage-designate tells them it would be better for them all to die than to surrender their women to the Turks. In the end, the heroic Piperi, after retreating to their mountain caves, succeed in driving back the Turks.

In the reckoning of victories and defeats, one inescapable fact emerges from this murky period: The Turks, no matter what force they applied to Montenegro, were incapable of stopping the Montenegrin quest for

Bishop Danilo Petrović

independence, much less of quelling the bravery of the people. In a practical sense, the Montenegrins, despite the terrible depredations of the Turks, must be regarded as an independent nation for much of the 17th century.

A Nation Once Again

The end of the 17th century was a turning point in the history of Turkey. The Venetians came up short-handed in the Peace of Karlowitz in 1699; along the Adriatic coast, they were able to keep only Risan and Novi and had to return the rest of their conquered territory to the Turks. On the other, hand Austria had decisively beaten the Turk back from the gates of Vienna, and the Ottoman Empire was like a gangrened limb—already beginning to smell of death. Its days were numbered even on the Adriatic coast.

But even if the Turkish army could be kept out of Montenegro, the problem of the Muslim converts would have remained. As the agents of the Ottoman Empire, these converts came increasingly into conflict with the Orthodox Christian clans. A symbolic Christian victory over the Muslims took place probably in 1707 (although it is traditionally dated to exactly 300 years ago in 1702). This victory over the Muslims, though an event of only local significance (in Djeklići), became a grand theme in folk poetry and the subject of *Gorski vijenac* (The Mountain Wreath), the literary masterpiece of Montenegro's greatest writer, Bishop Petar Petrović Njegoš.

The uprising against the Muslims was led by Danilo Šćepčević (later Petrović), who had been elected bishop in 1696, at the age of 20, and was consecrated by Serbian Patriarch Arsenije III Crnojević in 1700. It is fair to say that Danilo's accession marks the beginning of the history of modern Montenegro, the end of the period of Turkish domination and Montenegrin fragmentation, as surely as the flight of Djuradj Crnojević 200 years earlier marked the beginning. Bishop-Danilo came from the village of Njeguši, which lay about halfway between Kotor and Cetinje. The original inhabitants of the village had fled their homes in Hercegovina two centuries before. Bishop Danilo founded the Petrović-Njegoš dynasty and inaugurated the long and dramatic struggle for the establishment of an independent Serbian state in Montenegro.

Danilo's first step in reviving a country that had been besieged for 200 years and more recently devastated by Suleiman-pasha was to rebuild the church and the monastery in Cetinje. Recent experiences had taught him that the real threat to Montenegro did not come from the Turks but from the Montenegrin families that had converted to Islam. To take one small but significant example, Suleiman had made Rijeka Crnojevića an entirely Muslim village. Since this was the main market for trade between the mountains and the coast, Islamic control spelled economic isolation for Christians in the Montenegrin highlands.

Danilo's eyes may have been additionally opened by one instance of Islamic treachery. Under a safe conduct from the vizier of Scutari he was on his way to consecrate a church in Zeta, when he was set upon and captured by local Muslim converts who forced him to carry the pike on which he would be impaled—so they threatened—and took him to Podgorica, where they tortured him. The Montenegrins threatened reprisals but also offered to pay an enormous ransom of 3,000 ducats to the pasha for their bishop's life. The greedy pasha was deaf to the threats but happily accepted the bribe.

Upon his release the bishop began thinking about a solution to the question of converts. One Christmas Eve, he and the senior men of the country invited the converts to return to their ancestral faith, offering them the fatal choice—reconvert or die. The affair was, in fact, more of a war than a massacre, and many Christians met their death in the resulting skirmishes. Although reality is dwarfed by the legend, the event did mark the beginning of a process which would culminate in the disappearance of converts from Montenegro proper, though many remained along the coast, from Bar to Ulcinj and in the northern rim of Brda.

"We and the Russians are a hundred million strong"

It was during the rule of Bishop Danilo Montenegro first made significant contact with Orthodox Russia. Charles XII of Sweden, defeated in a war (1700-09) with Russia, fled to Constantinople, where he filled the head of Sultan Ahmed III with tales of the outnumbered Swedish troops defeating Russian armies many times their size. The Sultan scarcely needed a reason to turn his attention from Hungary, where the Turks had been badly beaten, to the apparently defenseless Russian Empire. In 1711, Peter responded to the Turkish invasion by calling on all Balkan Christians to unite in a war against Turkey.

Peter was already well into his project of westernizing Russia, and he had used the Orthodox Church's opposition to rapid modernization as an excuse to strip it of its privileges. The Orthodox hierarchy, particularly the Greeks, consequently viewed the Czar as a traitor. This may account for the fact that his appeal fell on deaf ears, except in Montenegro, of which he had learned from a Dubrovnik merchant named Sava Vladislavljević, who had translated Orbini's *Il Regno degli Slavi* into Russian.[5]

Peter sent two emissaries of Serbian birth, Col. Mihailo Miloradović, originally from Hercegovina, and Captain Ivan Lukačević, born in Podgorica. They arrived in Cetinje in the summer of 1711, bringing money and an "Imperial Charter" that recognized Montenegro's independence—168 years before the full international recognition granted at the Congress of Berlin. Czar Peter offered an alliance with Serbs, on the basis of ancient historical ties among the Slavs and in tribute to the Montenegrins' bravery. He invited them to rise up to defend their Orthodox faith and win their national freedom.

As soon as the proclamation was read, Bishop Danilo pledged the support of his people, and the Montenegrins, encouraged by the thought of having gained a powerful ally, went off to their homes to pick up supplies and ammunition, singing and shooting off guns as they went.[6] With Danilo's help, the Russians immediately organized the clans of Montenegro and Hercegovina for a major attack on Nikšić (which they failed to take), Spuž, and Gacko. The maritime republics of Venice and Dubrovnik did not support the campaign, however. Quite the contrary: Despite their protestations of neutrality they prevented the Serbs from obtaining the necessities of war. Unknown to Danilo, however, the Turkish army defeated the Russians on the northern shore of the Black Sea, and Peter signed a peace treaty in July 1711, even before the Montenegrin campaign had begun.

In the following year, Turkey was able to take revenge on Russia's ally, Montenegro, which they regarded as their own rebellious province. The sultan entrusted the punitive expedition to Ahmed-pasha, whose vastly superior army was driven back by the Montenegrins in a battle near Podgorica. Vojvoda Djurašković was killed and Vladika Danilo wounded, but other losses were insignificant. In 1713, however, the grand vizier arrived at the head of a much larger Turkish force. He invaded the country and battled his way to Cetinje in early August. Bishop Danilo, with some 500 men, was forced to retire to Hercegovina. The Turks plundered the Cetinje Monastery and forced some of the clans into submission. But fulfilling the old dictum that in Montenegro "small armies die, and large armies starve," the grand vizier was forced to withdraw his forces for a lack of supplies. The Montenegrins returned to banditry and guerrilla activity, harassing the Turks in any way they could.

In the summer of 1714, the Sublime Porte sent the Bosnian vizier, Numan-pasha Ćuprilić (Küprili), to Montenegro at the head of a major punitive expedition that was long remembered for the savage fury shown by his troops, who burned and plundered their way across the country. It was the Slavic-Muslim irregulars, the "Bashi-Bozuks" who displayed the worst cruelty, rather than the Turkish regulars. Wanting to "decapitate" the leadership, Ćuprilić invited 37 Montenegrin chieftains to a meeting in Hercegovina, giving his word of honor that they would be safe. When they arrived, they were arrested and later hanged. The dishonorable form of execution compounded the crime with an unforgivable insult that could only be washed away in blood. The now virtually leaderless Montenegrins, despite a fierce effort to resist the Turks, were soon overwhelmed. Bishop Danilo barely managed to escape to Russia in time, and about 2,300 of his people fled to Venetian territory.

In early 1716, Bishop Danilo returned from Russia, bringing money he had received from the emperor as a gift to the devastated Montenegrin families. Better than money was the news that Austria had entered another war against Turkey. This was particularly welcome in view of the intense pressure exerted by the viziers of Scutari and Bosnia on the Montenegrins to acknowledge their authority. They concentrated their attacks on the Brda, hoping to detach the Kuč and Piper clans from their alliance with Cetinje. Under intense pressure from two sides Danilo agreed to accept nominal Venetian rule as the price of independence from Turkey.

In early 1717, a delegation of headmen negotiated an agreement with Venice. In exchange for recognizing Venice as their protector, Montenegrins would enjoy home rule and maintain the rights of their Orthodox Church. Doge Cornaro agreed to excuse some customs duties at Kotor and to provide military and financial assistance. The republic also promised to pay salaries and pensions to a Montenegrin *guvernadur* (governor), as well as to various military leaders. A member of the Radonjić family of Njeguši bought the governorship from the first recipient of the honor, and the position—more ceremonial than real—became hereditary in the Radonjić family of Njeguši, just as the bishopric became hereditary in the rival Petrović family from the same village. Despite the lack of real power, the governorship established by Venice gave the appearance of divided authority and, for more than a century, offered an opportunity for outside interference into Montenegrin affairs.

Austria's war with Turkey sputtered to a close, and in the treaty of Požarevac, signed in July 1718, Montenegro's status as a nominal part of the Ottoman Empire was confirmed, though four of its communities (Majina, Pobor, Grbalj, and Brajić), were transferred to the Venetian Republic. This peace was maintained, with some short interruptions, until 1736, a year after Bishop Danilo's death.

Danilo, in both war and piece, proved himself to be a farsighted and patriotic statesman, as well as an inspired religious leader, defending his people in war, rebuilding churches the Turks had destroyed, and patiently constructing the institutions of religious and civic life. Far from being an isolated Montenegrin, he forged closer relations with Serbs engaged in the struggle for independence in regions controlled by Turkey and Austria. Even in a business transaction (the purchase of a Gospel), he referred to himself as "Danilo, the Cetinje Bishop Njegoš, the prince of the Serbian land." He also saw the wisdom in making an alliance with distant Russia and told his brother "I am Muscovite, a Muscovite, and again a Muscovite."[7]

While Austria and Russia battled Turkey in 1736, the Montenegrins—

Bishop Sava Petrović

at the insistence of the unwarlike Bishop Sava, who succeeded Danilo—kept their peace, or at least limited their aggression to routine banditry. Their posture was largely determined by the fact that Venice was in no condition for an all-out war with Turkey. Venice had not lost interest in Dalmatia, or no longer needed her Montenegrin allies, but Venetians were all too aware of their weakness in comparison with Russia and Austria. In making payments to individual headmen, the Venetians tried to buy the political influence their valor could not earn. Bishop Sava also fell under Venetian influence, but the effects of his bias were limited by his political incapacity, which soon became a cause for alarm. Sava would eventually be pressured into ceding his position to his cousin Vasilije Petrović. This somewhat irregular transfer of power made it clear that, contrary to Orthodox tradition, the bishop's miter had become hereditary in the House of Petrović.

The internal situation in Montenegro and an obviously altered ratio of forces between the Christian powers (Russia and Austria) and Turkey prompted Montenegro to launch a foreign political initiative. As an opening move, Bishop Sava had left for Russia (in 1742), seeking to renew the annual stipend to the Cetinje Monastery. It had not been paid since Peter's death, but Sava obtained it from Empress Elizabeth, who made a generous contribution of money, vestments, and religious books. The decision of Vasilije, the bishop's cousin, to go on his own to Venice (in 1744) precipitated a power struggle, which was only resolved by making Vasilije, as archimandrite, Sava's assistant and eventual replacement. Vasilije was consecrated bishop by Serbian Patriarch Atanasije in Belgrade in 1750. After the consecration, he left for Vienna, where he solicited Empress Maria Theresa's protection for Montenegro, but his request was not taken seriously.

After his unproductive mission to Vienna, Vasilije spent two years in Russia, vainly soliciting help for his people. To further his project, he wrote *A History of Montenegro*, a somewhat personal and slanted account of his people's history that was aimed more at political effect than strict accuracy. Returning from Russia with 5,000 rubles and more church books, the bishop found things in chaos. He set to work immediately on the long-term project of making his country free of both Turkey and Venice. The Turks (or rather the Montengrin converts in Scutari and Hercegovina) were the more pressing threat. When, in 1756, the Turks demanded, in addition to regular taxes, a tribute of 12 beautiful girls, Vasilije's refusal provoked the usual Turkish expedition of arson and destruction, which had no conclusive results. The Montenegrins might have been more successful if Venice had not blocked their attempts to acquire ammunition and gunpowder.

Struck again by wanderlust—and the need for further assistance—Vasilije returned to Russia late in the winter of 1758. The intrigues of his entourage coupled with his own eccentric proposals brought about his downfall. Suspicions arose over the financial aid given personally to

Vasilije and to the members of his entourage. He returned to Montenegro accompanied by Colonel Puchkov, who had orders to distribute 15,000 rubles among the Montenegrins and to report back to Russia on the situation. In the autumn of 1759, after several weeks in the country, Colonel Puchkov made his unflattering report: "The people are wild, they live in disorder, heads roll for the least offense, the clergy is grasping, the churches are deserted, and Russian assistance is distributed among the bishop's cousins." The bishop, perhaps in response to Russian criticism, began to mend his ways, enforcing the payment of taxes and improving the financial condition of the Cetinje Monastery. In 1765, he was back in Russia, seeking money and protection for his people from the new empress, Catherine II. Nothing came of his efforts, and Vasilije died suddenly in March 1766 in St. Petersburg, where he was buried.

Bishop Vasilije's reliance on Russia, a policy initiated by Bishop Danilo, left a lasting impression on Montenegrins, whose respect for the great Orthodox empire deepened into a loyal attachment and then into the reigning myth of the nation. The tiniest nation in the world and the greatest nation in Europe together formed, in the eyes of Montenegrins at least, an alliance of equals. "We and the Russians are 100 million strong." The trust that Serbs placed in Russia was not always rewarded. Time after time—most recently throughout the 1990's—the Russians have pursued their own interests, completely indifferent to the fate of their Serbian "brothers," and the worst of all legacies of the Russian alliance with Montenegro was the ready acceptance of communism as a "Russian" ideology.

Bishop Vasilije Petrović

Bishop Vasilije may have struck some people as avaricious and eccentric, but he spent most of the Russian money on making improvements to the Cetinje Monastery, now well established as a shrine for all Orthodox Christians in Montenegro, the Highlands (Brda), and Boka. After his death, however, Montenegro was plunged into chaotic conditions yet again. The crisis in authority was aggravated when the sultan, instigated by the Greek Orthodox hierarchy, decided to abolish the independent Serbian patriarchate and turn the Serbian Church over to the Greeks. The patriarch sought refuge in Cetinje, where he used his influence to strengthen the feeble authority of Sava, who was restored as vladika.

A Little Man Who Would Be King

On his last journey, Bishop Vasilije had taken with him his nephew Petar, who remained behind in Russia to secure an education that would be suitable to the future bishop and ruler of Montenegro. But in 1766, before young Petar returned to Montenegro with two Russian officers, a strange and mysterious man, endowed with alleged healing powers, settled in Majina, a Paštrović village just outside the walls of Budva. The stranger was well aware of the Montenegrins' strong attachment to Russia, and he may have encouraged them to start the fantastic rumor that he was none other than the Russian Emperor Peter III, Catherine the Great's husband who had been murdered four years earlier. The wild story was confirmed by Captain Marko Tancović, who had traveled in Russia with Bishop Vasilije and had met the real emperor at St. Petersburg. Simple people were greatly influenced by Tancović's words, especially when they discovered a similarity between the face of the healer and a painting in Podmajine Monastery, which was said (on who knows what authority) to be a portrait of Peter III.

The stranger was soon known as Czar Šćepan Mali (Stephen the Small, Stefanino Piccolo in Venetian sources). From far and near the chiefs came to see and hear him. His arrival in Montenegro, at a time of widespread banditry and tribal anarchy, seemed a godsend. Unlike most impostors, Šćepan proved to be a wise and effective ruler. Asked to say positively who he was, Šćepan told the Montenegrins he would only reveal his identity once they had made peace among themselves. When the clans responded to his request by signing a temporary armistice, he tore up the paper, telling them he had ordered peace and not a mere truce. When the clans actually did make peace, he could not avoid making a statement. He declared that, indeed, he was the emperor, that he had miraculously escaped from the daggers of his assassins and, after a long sea voyage, landed on the Adriatic shore because he knew of the Montenegrins' bravery and loyalty. He declared that he had no desire to return to Russia and no greater wish than to help Montenegro strengthen its independence.

With the support of the vojvode, Šćepan established his court at Njeguši, where he presided over the assembly and received foreign dignitaries. He also imposed a severe judicial discipline upon his subjects, who were all too much inclined to anarchy. Although he had probably met the real Petar III in Russia, Bishop Sava did not dare express suspicions about Šćepan's identity. Sava did, however, inform the Russian envoy in Constantinople about the appearance of the "Russian Czar." The envoy replied that the man was an impostor. The bishop sent copies of this reply around the nahije, instigating a controversy from which Šćepan emerged victorious, even to the point of having the bishop held under house arrest for several weeks.

The growing independence of Šćepan's regime and the energy he displayed alarmed both Venice and Russia. The Venetians decided to act when they learned that Šćepan's supporters had mounted an uprising in Risan against Venetian control, and the republic characteristically offered a reward to anyone who would poison Šćepan. Empress Catherine II, confident in Russia's prestige with her ally, asked the Montenegrins to expel the impostor. The impostor's authority nevertheless grew. He punished crime severely and even dared shoot two Montenegrins for theft—an unprecedented act that left a deep impression on the people. Such was the fear he inspired that no one ventured to touch a purse and a silver-mounted pistol that he left for weeks by the side of the busy road between Cetinje and Kotor. Šćepan established courts of justice, prohibited work on Sunday, ordered a census of all men fit to bear arms, and embarked on an ambitious road-building program that eventually brought him grave injuries when an explosive charge went off prematurely during the construction of a road from Cetinje to Budva.

The Turks, believing that Šćepan was a Russian agent in disguise, took a more direct approach than the Venetians had and organized a fresh expedition. They attacked from three sides with a force of 60,000, this time confident that Venice would not help their erstwhile clients. Under the command of Bosnian Vizier Osman-pasha, the Turkish army launched its main assault against the area of Nikšić. The Montenegrin force of 2,000, accompanied by Šćepan, met the Turks in the Ostrog Pass in early September 1768. The superior Turkish army won a swift victory, and Šćepan, who had not distinguished himself in battle, escaped to safety—an act of cowardice that no genuine Montenegrin could commit. But the elements were on the side of the mountaineers: The Montenegrins fortuitously gained a supply of ammunition when lightning struck an ammunition depot on November 1, and the Turks withdrew. The people saw in this delivery the act of Providence, and the bard who immortalized this victory called on his brothers-in-arms to "believe in the one God from whom the men of Crna Gora receive joy, courage, and health."

The outbreak of another war between Russia and Turkey took some of the immediate pressure off Montenegro. The Russians sent Prince George Vladimirović Dolgoruki, with ample supplies and war materiel, to ask the Montenegrins to join the war against the Turks, which the empress had just declared—and to repudiate the impostor. When Šćepan was confronted by his Russian accuser, he admitted the fraud but claimed that he was motivated by the desire to save Montenegro and professed respect and loyalty for the empress. The vojvode explained to the Russian envoy that they did not really know who Šćepan was, but they did know that only he could keep order and unite the clans against their enemies. Dolgoruki reluctantly came to see their point; he even conferred the rank of a Russian officer on the false Peter, appointing him imperial regent and instructing the chieftains to obey him as before. Although his prestige declined, Šćepan was able to rule in peace for five more years until, in 1774, he was strangled by his own servant, a Greek, who was allegedly in the pay of Mahmud-pasha, ruler of Scutari. By a curious irony he died in exactly the same way as the unfortunate emperor whose identity he had assumed.

Šćepan Mali, impostor though he was, had taught the Montenegrins a valuable lesson. If they were content to go on killing each other in endless cycles of outrage and vengeance, they would never muster the strength to drive the Turks out of the land they occupied. Šćepan accomplished what no Montenegrin leader had managed in several centuries: He had united his people, taught them respect for law and order, and prepared them for the coming struggle against the invaders.

Notes

For the period between the fall of the Crnojevići and the rise of Petar I Njegoš, I have relied heavily on the older works of Popović and Gopčević. The vivid and sometimes polemical books of Medaković still breathe the mountain air of Montenegro and provide many telling details.

1. Miller, William. *The Balkans* (London, 1896).

2. Fleming, *Politics*.

3. McNeill, p. 52.

4. Gopčević, pp. 149ff. Stephenson, pp. 115-16. The struggle over Mantova absorbed Europe's attention for years and provides the historical setting for Manzoni's *I Promessi sposi*.

5. For Peter's problems with the Orthodox, see Summers.

6. For Peter the Great and Montenegro, see Gopčević, pp. 170ff., Popović pp. 89ff., Medaković p. 45.

7. Medaković, (1895), p. 19.

THE STONY ROAD TO STATEHOOD

Oh, da mi je očima vidjeti
Crna Gora izgub na namiri!
Tad bi mi se upravo činilo
Da mi sv'jetli kruna Lazareva
E sletio Miloš medju Srbe.

If only I could see with my own eyes Crna Gora at peace! Then it would really seem that the crown of Lazar shines with glory, that Miloš comes back to earth among the Serbs.

—Bishop Peter II Petrović Njegoš

By the closing decades of the 18th century, little had changed in Montenegro. The roughly 120,000 people were still living out their lives, much as their ancestors had done, scratching out a subsistence in 240 or so village communities distributed among the 36 tribes. The occasional wandering Parisian or Londoner who landed in Montenegro must have thought he was Odysseus in the land of the Cyclopes, where each man ruled as patriarch over his wife and children. The usual frictions between the Montenegrin clans were aggravated during this period by rivalry between the Petrović family, which gave the country its bishops, and the Radonjići, which monopolized the position of *guvernadur*. With the departure of Šćepan the Small from the scene, the rivalry became acute, and both sides sought to gain the goodwill of the Russian court.

Before his death in 1782, Bishop Sava had found a new ally for his people: Austria. In 1779, he signed a treaty with Maria Theresa, which treated Montenegro as a virtually independent country and stipulated that, in the event of a Turkish withdrawal from Serbia, the whole of Zeta (down to the Bojana River) along with Hercegovina and the Brda should be united with Crna Gora.[1] Sava died in 1782, and although he had arranged for the elevation of his nephew (Arsenije Plamenac), Sava's cousin

Petar, who had already proved himself to be an able assistant, was made his successor.

Petar was a man of very different stamp from his predecessor. An energetic ruler, as bold in war as he was persuasive in the council chamber, he was the first Montenegrin ruler to gain European recognition for his small mountain state. The greatest European powers—Austria, Russia, and England—did not scorn to accept, or even to solicit, his aid. His rude, untrained forces held the armies of the great Napoleon in check, and he excelled his sworn enemy, the French emperor, in his heroic effort to codify his country's laws and ensure their enforcement. Napoleon, after all, was merely building on a thousand years of French statecraft and legislation, while Petar had to start from the anarchy of wild mountaineers, whose only law was the *krvna osveta* (blood feud).

Blood revenge (and the feud it may inspire), though it is not much understood in the 20th century, is a nearly universal human phenomenon, which is portrayed in some of the greatest literature of the West: Homer's *Iliad* and *Odyssey*, *Beowulf*, *Hamlet*, and *Huckle-berry Finn*. As the Old Testament, in laying down a set of rules, makes clear, revenge is not so much a desire as a duty. If a member of my family is murdered, there is a stain on every member until the blood is either purged by ritual and compensation or washed away in more blood. The Greeks called this blood pollution *agos*.

Bishop Petar I Petrović

It is not only the Greeks who felt a stain as a wound. In the Montenegrin understanding of *krvna osveta*, the relative of a slain man felt the eye of the community upon him, expecting him to do the right thing, and the sense of the community became the voice of conscience. According to a not entirely sympathetic non-Montenegrin Serb, *osveta*

> is something born into a man. It has to do with wounds to the soul and the heart. A Montenegrin says that he would rather die than live his life shamefully . . . When he seeks vengeance, the *osvetnik* (vengeance-taker) knows whom it is he will kill and why he will kill him . . . he cannot work, nor sleep in peace, until he has fulfilled his evil and blood mission . . . When a Montenegrin takes vengeance, then he is happy; then it seems to him that he has been born again . . . [2]

The moral burden of revenge does not derive from an abstract code of justice but from the reality of kinship, and despite the apparent bloody-mindedness of the revenge-seeker, the underlying motives have more to do with a man's intimate sense of belonging to his family or clan than with hatred of the killer.

In a Montenegrin feud, the injured family has the right to besiege the house of an enemy who belongs to the same clan. A successful siege results in the departure of the family both from the house and the clan. More often, once honor has been served, a negotiated settlement can be made. Struggles between clans were carried out as wars, though there were similar laws even for clan wars. The siege is only used against the house of a fellowtribesman, because it is aimed at exile rather than mass homicide. Around the world, the rules of engagement for blood feuds forbade the killing of women, children, and the elderly, and the purpose—paradoxical as this may seem—was the restoration of order, not the fulfillment of bloodlust. But while blood revenge may serve the needs of a kin-based society, it is a decided inconvenience when a society needs to display a united front against an enemy as resourceful and determined as the Ottoman Empire (or Venice, France, or Austria). Vladika Petar would have his hands full, in trying to repress the feuding spirit of the clans.

Petar set off for Russia, where he hoped to be consecrated as bishop, but unable to obtain an Austrian passport for the trip, he went instead to the Serbian Metropolitan in Karlowitz, where (after a six months' delay brought about by a broken arm), Metropolitan Mojsije Putnik made him Vladika in 1784.

In the meantime, a new vizier had come to power in Scutari, Mahmud-pasha of the Bushatli family (a branch of the Crnojevići). The vizier, who had arranged the murder of Šćepan Mali, almost immediately embarked upon the ambitious project of making himself a virtually independent ruler in the western Balkans. To accomplish his purpose, Mahmud-pasha would defy the sultan, even as he was simultaneously attempting to extend his power over the Montenegrins. Vladika Petar learned of his plans for attacking Montenegro and set out for Russia to ask for help. His well-laid plans were foiled by Prince Potemkin, Catherine's advisor and lover. Potemkin was at odds with the bishop's Russian patron, and he ordered Petar to leave St. Petersburg within 24 hours.

Mahmud-pasha did attack Montenegro in the spring of 1785. Taking advantage of the disorders and feuding, the vizier easily broke the disorganized resistance, and after capturing Cetinje, he put the monastery and about 100 houses to the torch before going on to plunder and massacre the Paštrović clan. Venice assisted the invasion by blocking the Montenegrins' supply routes, and to drive home the point, the governor of Kotor congratulated Mahmud-pasha on his success.

On his return from Russia, the bishop found the country in a state of devastation and confusion. The people were reduced to eating grass and bark, and all Montenegro, except Katunska nahija, was paying tribute to the vizier. The vladika had a difficult task in front of him: to reestablish peace among the feuding clans and to persuade them to stop paying tribute.

The Turks had problems of their own. Mahmud-pasha was by now in rebellion against the sultan, and another war had broken out between Turkey and Russia (allied with Austria). Both the Austrians and the Russians asked Montenegro to enter the war. Petar hesitated, observing that Montenegro had little to gain from such a conflict, especially since the Austrian emissary Brugniard was simultaneously courting the rebellious vizier of Scutari. The bishop refused a transparent offer of a bribe until the Russians advised him to assist the Austrians.

The new Austrian representative went to Scutari, against Petar's advice, to arrange an alliance with Muhmad-pasha. The agreement was signed, and gifts were exchanged, but having learned of Turkish successes in the field, Mahmud-pasha sent a party of Albanians to attack the delegation. The Austrian emissary was decapitated, and the vizier sent his head to Constantinople as a peace offering to the sultan.

The greater war, in the meantime, was dragging on to its inconclusive conclusion. Though the allies were able to take Belgrade, mutual suspicions resulted in a peace (of Sistova in 1792) that returned their territories to the *status quo ante*. The sultan was eager to smooth relations with Serbs in Serbia, who had supported Austria, and granted them a semi-autonomous territory around Belgrade, which would be the nucleus of the future Serbian state.

The Turks were less inclined to placate Montenegro, and in 1796 Mahmud-pasha led another expedition, in which he was defeated and wounded in land of the Martinići. Undaunted, he returned to Montenegro at the head of an army of as many as 30,000 troops under the leadership of seven French officers. The crucial battle was fought in a narrow pass near the village of Kruse on September 22 of the same year. The Montenegrin army, led by the sword-wielding bishop and the *guvernadur*, won a splendid victory. Mahmud-pasha himself was taken prisoner and executed. His head was sent to Cetinje, where curious visitors today may still contemplate the renegade's skull and meditate on the fortunes of war.

In rousing his people to fight, Bishop Petar had appealed to their courage as Montenegrins and to their Serbian identity:

> We came to show the enemy of our faith, our name, and the freedom we hold dear, that we are Montenegrins, that we are a people . . . willing to fight for our freedom till the last drop of blood . . . we do not allow the damned enemy of Christianity to get through these free and beloved mountains alive, the mountains for which our great-grandfathers, our grandfathers, our fathers and we ourselves have spilled our blood. Then take up arms and on the bloody field of battle . . . show the enemy what free mountains are capable of. Show that an immortal Serb heart beats within our chests, and Serb blood bubbles.

The Vladika's prestige was enhanced by these victories over the Turks, and he tried to exert his augmented authority by imposing order on the rebellious clans. One sign of hope was the decision of the Brda clans (Piperi and Bjelopavlići) to unite formally with Montenegro.

The bishop traveled the country, making peace and calling for reconciliation, and he began drawing up laws that would put an end to the bloodfeuds that were so much a part of Montenegrin life. He had some success, notably in drawing up a *Zakonik* (law code) and securing its approval in the assembly. The progress, however, was more symbolic than real, and the clans went on as before, seeking justice by the sword and refusing to pay the taxes for the support of the new judges who were being appointed. "Better to pay tribute to the vizier than to the bishop," some complained. Part of Bishop Petar's failure to impose order may have derived from the saint's reluctance to use violence against his own people. It was not a mistake that would be repeated by his successors.

Despite its rugged isolation, Montenegro could not avoid the turmoils that broke out in the late 18th century: the French Revolution and the wars it engendered, and the rise and fall of Napoleon Bonaparte, whose impact on Europe was more like that of a natural catastrophe than of a political or military career. For the Montenegrins, the most significant event was the fall of the Venetian Republic. Venice passed to Austrian control in 1797 under the Treaty of Campo Formio. The Montenegrins had moved in to reoccupy some of the coastal territory, including Budva, but they were forced to relinquish their gains, and Boka Kotorska became a bone of contention between Montenegro and Austria.

Venice had been at best an unreliable ally, but her loss of independence forced Montenegro to seek new friends. Despite 20 years of poor relations, Vladika Petar asked the Russian court for financial assistance and proposed a plan for reorganizing the Montenegrin state under Russian auspices. Emperor Paul agreed only to give the Cetinje Monastery 4,000 rubles and clerical vestments and books valued at 2,200 rubles. In January 1799, an Imperial Charter arrived, confirming all the previous charters, promising the assistance of the Russian fleet and an annual stipend of 1,000 ducats.

The gifts and promises should have been an indication of improved relations, but the new Czar Alexander I was annoyed with Bishop Petar for continuing to have relations with France. The task of taking the independent-minded bishop out of the game was entrusted to Lieutenant-General Count Marko Ivelić (of Risan). Ivelić arrived in 1804 with an imperial charter, a charter from the Synod of the Russian Church, and a personal letter from the emperor. All the documents were highly critical of the bishop's political and spiritual leadership. Ivelić, however, overplayed his hand, and not content with presenting the unflattering documents, he spread slander about the bishop and stirred up dissension. The Montenegrins rejected his arguments and demanded that a "real Russian" should be sent. The new Russian emissary, who came to Kotor in August 1804, was able to reach a face-saving compromise by blaming all problems on the bishop's intriguing secretary, Fra Francisco Dolci de Vicković. The friar was sentenced to death, then pardoned, then found dead in prison—strangled, so one story went, by the cincture (rope) used to tie up his Franciscan habit.

Napoleon's battles and victories had their effect also on Montenegro. Baron Rukavina, the Austrian admiral, wrote to Petar, asking him to use his influence with the people of the Boka on behalf of the power, which had assisted him with ammunition in his recent campaign. But scarcely had the Austrian admiral entered the coveted Bay when a French fleet arrived off Dubrovnik and ordered the Austrians to withdraw from Boka. In his distress, the Austrian commander applied again to Petar, urging him to join against the common enemy, and even offering to serve under his command. The czar seconded the request of his ally, and sent a special envoy to Montenegro to enlist the support of its ruler against Napoleon. But before the vladika had taken the field, the Peace of Pressburg, which was concluded after the defeat at Austerlitz, formally consigned Boka Kotorska to France. The Austrian commissioner at Kotor announced that in six weeks' time, he would hand over the forts.

The Montenegrins and the leaders in the communities of Boka were opposed to the French takeover. In Kotor and Dubrovnik, however, there were young radicals who supported the French Revolution, but their dreams were dashed when the French officers stripped the churches of gold and silver and drafted the monks into the army. In Dubrovnik, the French "suspended" the city's chartered liberties and replaced the republic's flag with the French tricolor. French arrogance only further aroused the population, and with the support of Russia, which sent several ships to Boka, the Montenegrins and Bokelji seized Konavle and Cavtat and laid siege to the French in Dubrovnik.

The Montenegrins were not daunted by the name of Napoleon. Aided by their Russian allies, they defeated the French in a four days' engagement, and Dubrovnik would inevitably have fallen into their hands had not orders arrived from the Czar that Boka should be surrendered to the Austrians. As usual, the brave mountaineers found that they had been duped. Disgusted by this treatment, the Vladika withdrew from the siege. But the guerilla warfare that followed was conducted with the utmost savagery by his subjects and the people of the coast. No quarter was shown on either side.

The Treaty of Tilsit (July 1807) confirmed the French possession of Boka. In 1810, French-controlled "Illyria" was divided into seven provinces, including Dalmatia, whose capital was Zara, and Albania, with a capital at Dubrovnik. This scheme may have been merely a cartographic fantasy drawn up by Napoleon's bureaucracy or a deliberate attempt to quench national aspirations by imposing borders that made no ethnic sense (Albanians, Serbs, and Croats lived within Albania, while Croats were divided), but it had the unintended consequence of encouraging a sense of South Slavic unity. From this perspective, Napoleon was the father of Yugoslavia.

Relations between France and Montenegro went from bad to worse. Although Napoleon's representatives did improve the treatment of the Orthodox and provided money for a seminary, French officers openly despised the Montenegrins as savages. When General Marmont invited Bishop Petar to a meeting in Kotor, his people were so suspicious that they insisted upon accompanying their leader to the fortress and stationed themselves outside with drawn knives, telling the Vladika, that if the French tried anything funny, he should throw the general out the window, and they would finish him off with their knives. Marmont was furious and denounced both the Montenegrins and their Russian backers as savages who decapitated their prisoners, and he asked the bishop why he could not be content to be a priest instead of a ruler. "Savages?" asked the bishop. It was not Montenegrins who dragged their king through the streets and murdered him. Although the meeting was stormy, in his memoir General Marmont confessed that he had been impressed by the intelligence and nobility of the handsome Serbian bishop.[3]

The bishop's response was a fair retort, but the French had never fought an enemy quite so savage as the Montenegrins. The story that the Montenegrins played bowls with the heads of the French soldiers and remarked how lightheaded their enemies were may be invention—though not an unbelievable one. But there is no doubt that they decapitated the French general, Delgorgues, who had been made a prisoner. In the frequent skirmishes that took place, the French soldiers were no match for the mountainbands, which harassed them on all sides, though the French were to display their own version of savagery. Montenegrins, even in their deadliest bloodfeuds (including the Christmas Eve attack on the renegades) killed only men and spared women, children, and the elderly. But when a group of shepherds from Njeguši wanted to bring their flocks peacefully into French territory and, to avoid armed conflict, put the women in front, French soldiers did not hesitate to shoot a woman.

General Marmont, frustrated in his military attempts to reduce the Montenegrins to obedience, tried a series of ploys to insert French influence into Montenegro (sending a consul, offering to build a road, trying to establish a garrison in Podmajine Monastery, which was under the bishop's authority), all of which anticipate later attempts to establish an "international" presence in Yugoslavia. Napoleon was furious at the rejection of his overtures and vowed that he would lay waste to the country with fire and sword, until its name became Monte Rosso instead of Montenegro, the Red Mountain instead of the Black.

The French resolved upon a direct attack in 1811 and gained the vizier of Scutari as an ally. The arrival of the English fleet, however, changed the dynamics, especially when the Montenegrins learned that England and Russia were on the same side. With help from an English fleet commanded by Sir William Hoste, the Montenegrins drove back the Turks and defeated the French, who were forced to take refuge in Kotor.

In early January 1814, the French surrendered Kotor, and for a brief interval Montenegro had access to the sea. Bishop Petar thought the time was ripe to seek Russian approval for annexing Boka to Montenegro. The peoples of Montenegro, Brda, and Boka reached an agreement on a mutual defense pact, but while the bishop's representative was on his way to St. Petersburg, the Catholics of Boka were sending an emissary to Vienna to request the emperor to make Boka a part of his empire. Their wish became reality when the Treaty of Paris of was signed in May 1814, giving Boka to Austria. The preference of some Bokelji for Austrian rule did not indicate hostility against their Orthodox neighbors. The region had become predominantly Serbian over the years, and Catholics and Orthodox mixed and intermarried freely.

Although the people of Boka have maintained a pronounced Mediterranean identity that would tend to separate them from the Serbs of the mountains, their historic connection with the Nemanjići, who visited often, was preserved. The Grbljani in particular were intensely proud of their Serbian heritage, claiming even that their name derives from Prince Lazar's surname (which they rendered Grbljanović). In the 19th century, the Bokelji celebrated St. Sava's day (according to Simo Matavulj). When in 1848, Bishop Peter II Njegoš advised the Bokelji to join Croatia, they refused, declaring "we are Serbs."

The Vladika was said to be sad over his failure to unite Boka to Montenegro, but he had other causes for melancholy. If Montenegro was too weak to advance her frontier to the sea, the country was also incapable of playing a meaningful part in the Serbian uprisings that broke out in 1804.

Although the Serbs in both Serbia and Hercegovina expected Montenegro's help against Turkey, the bishop had been instructed by Russia to keep out of the fighting. Karadjordje, the leader of the Serb rebels, reproached him for failing to "be of great help and support to the Serbian people in their liberation." When Russia joined the war, Montenegro was free to participate, and together with the Serbs in Hercegovina, Montenegro attacked the Turks in Nikšić and Klobuk, but without success.

Although Karadjordje again appealed in 1809 to Bishop Petar, asking him "to show your love for Christianity by attacking the enemy and advancing to us and raising all Christian brothers in order that we should all join forces and attack the infidel enemy from all sides," military cooperation between Serbia and Montenegro, for all of Saint Petar's good wishes, did not materialize. Although the sultan's internationally recognized supremacy over Serbia naturally dictated a cautious policy toward Turkey, the bishop never wavered in his support for Serbian liberation. In a poem, he compares Karadjorje with the great Serbian heroes and describes "Djuro Petrović" as the one who has "snatched his beloved mother from the devil's jaws." Petar I concludes his encomium with the hope that Serbs will go on to drive the Turks from Bosnia and Hercegovina and unite with Crna Gora.

The Serbs' general misfortune was compounded by an earthquake in Montenegro in 1817 and by a plague epidemic that broke out the following year. The long years of war and blockade took their toll, and by 1816, the country was suffering from famine. Without resources, the Vladika could only send hundreds of families into exile in Russia and Serbia. The vizier of Bosnia attacked Montenegro in 1820, but he was defeated.

Coming to the end of his life, Bishop Petar made a last effort to bring peace to the clans, and in the Narodna Skupština in 1830, he made a farewell speech calling for reconciliation. He died that very night, leaving behind a passionate plea for peace, asking the heroes to live in peace, saying farewell to the "free mountains," and asking God's blessings on the Montenegrins and their "Serb kin." Petar had been viewed as a saint even within his life, and when, four years after his death, his tomb was opened and the body found to be uncorrupted, his successor made his sainthood official.

Bishop Petar II Njegoš: The Creation of a State

Bishop Petar I was succeeded by his nephew Rade, who was only 17 years old. In 1823, the assembly had approved Petar I's choice of his nephew Djordje, who turned out to prefer a career in the military rather than the Church. Vienna, the successor to Venetian ambitions in Montenegro, leaped upon this chance to meddle and sought help from the Radonjići. The Guvernadur Vuk Radonjić said openly that the Petrovići had reigned long enough and that it was time for a change. The Petrović family discussed the matter with the clan chieftains, and together they settled on a second nephew, Rade son of Tomo, who was designated as heir in Bishop Petar's will. When the will was read, Guvernadur Vuk Radonjić stood up and, in a gesture that was as futile as it was potentially destructive, opposed the decision and declared his support for Djordje.

Accepted enthusiastically both by the leading clergy and by the chieftains, Rade was consecrated as Petar II, metropolitan of Montenegro and the Coastlands in St. Petersburg in 1833, in the presence of Emperor Nicholas I of Russia. Vladika Petar II is known to history as Njegoš, the family's surname taken from their home village of Njeguši (a name also used by his uncle St. Petar). Bishop Njegoš is undoubtedly the most remarkable man produced by this nation of remarkable men, and though he lived in the smallest country in Europe, he was among the most brilliant men of the 19th century. Like his predecessors, he was a statesman as well as a bishop, but he was also one of the greatest writers (if not the greatest) in the history of the Serbian language.

In taking power, Njegoš undertook two major tasks: In foreign policy, he strengthened the security of Montenegro by supporting the Turkish beis who had rebelled against the authority of the Turkish state; at home, he had to consolidate his personal authority while establishing the governmental apparatus necessary to a functioning state.

The young Bishop Petar II Petrović Njegoš was not above concocting a political fiction when it suited his purpose. At this time, there arrived from Russia a Serb named Ivanović, who was born in Podgorica but had inherited a wealthy estate in Russia. Knowing the esteem in which the czar was held, the bishop persuaded Ivanović to represent himself as an emissary from the czar, and the two conspirators concocted a fraudulent Russian document, affixing the seal of a charter sent to Petar I, and even had a Russian general's uniform made in Kotor. (There were apparently no tailors in Montenegro, and if there were one, he might have talked.)

Ivanović then publicly informed the people of Montenegro of the czar's confidence in young Rade.[4] Even before going to Russia, Njegoš (with help, again, from the mysterious Ivanović) created three central organs of state power: the Praviteljstvujušći Senat (Governing Senate), which was an assembly of principal clan leaders, presided over by the Vladika, with judicial and executive as well as legislative functions; the Guardia, an executive body of 388 members that implemented the Senate's decisions and functioned as a lower court; and the *Perjanici*, 30 plume-helmeted special police, who guarded the bishop and Senate and arrested (and punished) enemies of the state.

Shortly after the establishment of the government, Njegoš imposed the first regular system of taxation as part of the Zakoni Otačastva (Laws of the Nation), drawn up with the help of Ivanović. Every household was to pay one thaler a year per hearth. Collection of this tax was resisted by many Montenegrins, who resented any infringement of their liberty. Njegoš's innovations were bound to spark conflict, and any resistance was sure to be led by the Petrovići's traditional rivals, the Radonjić family from which the guvernadur was selected. Vuk had never accepted the elevation of Rade and was circulating a not impossible story that the old bishop's will was a forgery. Worse, he was intriguing with Austria, which insisted upon communicating only with the guvernadur.

Bishop Petar II Petrović

Unluckily, his secret correspondence with Austria fell into the hands of the Vladika, who wasted little time in divesting (in 1830) Vuk Radonjić of his governorship, "because he has dared, without consulting anybody or obtaining permission, to write to somebody and arrange secret meetings and agreements." Less than two years later, he and the entire Radonjić family were banished from the country and their houses burnt to the ground. The office of guvernadur, which had caused so much trouble, was abolished.

Njegoš, although a devout Christian and deeply spiritual poet, did not believe in half measures against "the breakers of general peace, who have received their just deserts . . . I have destroyed this savagery, established peace and quiet guaranteed life and property to all." As a result, said the bishop, he was loved throughout the country.

Vladika Rade, as he was sometimes affectionately known, was especially harsh against those who defied his orders. Marko, a bold hajduk of the Djilas clan (a tiny offshoot of the Vojnovići), went to work for the bishop for several years. Sent to escort two Turks, who had come to Cetinje on official business, he could not resist the temptation to rob and kill the enemies of his people. An earlier ruler might have forgiven this "peccadillo," but not Njegoš, who declared him an outlaw. Marko outlived the bishop, however, and composed a satiric song about his death.[5]

The Turks, by their provocations and attacks, gave Montenegro the opportunity to strengthen its claim to independence. In 1832, a Turkish invasion of Brda was hurled back by the Piperi, and Njegoš tried to reap the reward of his victory by attacking Podgorica. The attempted liberation failed because of a lack of troops. The Vladika faced an equally serious challenge from the vizier of Hercegovina, Ali-pasha Stočević Rizvanbegović, who in 1836 defeated the Montenegrins and Hercegovinians and seized the disputed town of Grahovo.

The fighting over Grahovo had made Smail-aga Čengić of Gacko a hero among the Muslims. Smail-aga, together with his son, was notorious for his reign of terror over the Serbs, which ultimately proved his undoing. In the autumn of 1840, he was murdered in the Drobnjaci. This event provoked an expedition by Ali-pasha, which was countered by a Montenegrin force led personally by Bishop Petar II. After great loss of life on both sides, Vladika Petar and Ali-pasha normalized relations in 1842, when the Pashaluk of Bosnia and Hercegovina signed a treaty with the "independent region of Montenegro." The treaty did not bring peace with the Turks, since, at virtually the same time as the treaty was being signed, the vizier of Scutari attacked the Piperi and, after an initial repulse, seized two islands in Lake Scutari and began harassing Montenegrin fishermen and depriving them of their livelihood.

The conflict dragged on despite Russian and Austrian attempts at mediation, and Montenegro was attacked repeatedly by the viziers of Scutari and Hercegovina, both of whom were Serbs. Bishop Petar wrote both viziers a letter, appealing to their common blood and calling upon them to fight alongside of their Serb brothers. Although the vizier of Scutari was offended by the letter and continued to harass the Montenegrins, Ali-pasha Stočević, who entered into correspondence with the vladika, was moved to tell the Muslims of his district that Njegoš was a real Serbian leader from the time of Kosovo.

Njegoš's devotion to Serbia and Kosovo found its highest expression in his literary masterpiece, *Gorski vijenac* (*The Mountain Wreath*), a poem commemorating Bishop Danilo's campaign against the Muslim converts. But although the poem takes place in Montenegro in the early 18th century, the real subject is the struggle for Serbian independence, which had been going on since the end of the 14th century. In fact, the work is dedicated to the ashes of the Father of Serbia, that is, to Karadjordje, whom he compares with the greatest men of the 19th century.

Throughout the work, which is written in the form of a Greek tragedy, complete with choruses (recast as Serbian kola (dances), Njegoš asks the Serbs to live up to the model set by the heroes of Kosovo, especially Miloš Obilić, who killed the sultan in his tent. Kosovo is the ever-present backdrop, as if the battle had taken place in the generation of Danilo's father. "We were both at Kosovo," an Orthodox Serb says pointedly to one of the converts, "but I have been faithful, while you are a traitor." Obviously, neither Serb was at a battle which had taken place three centuries earlier, but all true Serbs, in a mystical sense, were at Kosovo, and (as the Orthodox Serb proclaims in the poem), they fought the enemy there, and they fight him now. The sultan offered wealth and power to Serbs who renounced their faith and converted to Islam, and some (like Stefan Crnojević) accepted the offer. Similar offers have been made to every generation of Montenegrins, by Turks, Venetians, Austrians, and representatives of "the international community," who wish to divide the Serbs and keep them weak.

Over and over in the poem, Njegoš warns the Serbs not to divide their forces in the face of an enemy—a classic military mistake. In the first *kolo*, the singers tell us that God is punishing the Serbs for their sins, because their leaders fought each other. Anarchy and faithlessness were the fruits of discord.

The merciful Danilo still does not want to kill brother Montenegrins and tries to remind the Muslims of their Serbian heritage (as the poet did in his letter to the viziers), but the converts answer with mockery. A cup cannot hold two drinks, as one of them observes, and while the Muslim paradise is filled with blue-eyed Houri, all Christianity can offer is the dead wood of the Cross and the story of Miloš Obilić. The quarrel between Cross and Crescent in the Balkans has not been settled to this day, though an isolated Montenegro might easily turn into another Kosovo.

Bishop Petar, while fending off the almost annual Muslim raids, also had to deal with Austria, which was continuing to intrigue its way into power in the Balkans. The Hapsburg bureaucracy, however, had no easy time finding its way through the maze of feuds and quarrels among the clans under their authority, much less to sort out relations with the Montenegrins and Hercegovinians. The long-standing dispute over the Podmajine and Stanjević Monasteries (extraterritorial possessions) was resolved when Bishop Petar II sold them to Austria.

Although Montenegrins complained about the loss of territory for mere money, the regularization of the border between Montenegro and Austria led to improved relations between the two countries and amounted to a *de facto* recognition of a Montenegrin sovereign state independent of Turkish authority. This arrangement, however, constituted a confession of one of the bishop's greatest failures: Montenegro was even more removed from the access to the coast that would have made commercial progress possible.

The extreme poverty and ever-present threat of famine forced Njegoš, as much as his predecessors, to rely on Russian financial assistance. The bishop visited the Russian court in St. Petersburg in May 1837 (after a detour to Paris which scandalized some Montenegrins back home). The good impression he made upon the court did much to dispel the web of scandal and intrigue that his enemies had woven. Czar Nicholas I not only increased his annual assistance to Montenegro from 1,000 ducats to 9,000 but also responded positively to future requests.

With Russian assistance, Bishop Petar II was able to make substantial improvements in Montenegro, whose economy, education, and infrastructure had remained virtually unchanged since the days of Ivan Crnojević. Livestock breeding was still the most common form of livelihood, though potatoes, introduced from Russia by the bishop, were becoming an important crop. The still-frequent famines were alleviated by wheat imported from Russia and by food bought with Russian (and some Serbian) money.

It was only during Njegoš's time that roads and schools began to be built on a regular basis. Šćepan Mali's short-lived program of road construction was abandoned after his death.

Since only the priests were literate, Njegoš sent the first groups of boys to be educated in Boka and Russia. The first school was opened in Cetinje in 1834. Njegoš had a small printing shop, where he printed his own works, as well as schoolbooks and the five annual editions of the "Grlica" (Dove) Almanac. Unfortunately, the type eventually had to be melted down for bullets.

Njegoš closely followed the uprisings in the South Slavic lands during the revolutionary year 1848. A rebellion in Venice against Austrian rule resulted in the temporary reestablishment of the republic, and the example of Venice was an inspiration throughout the Hapsburg domains. Montenegrins were not eager to see the return of Venetian rule to the coast, and Bishop Petar, in addition to offering military assistance to Croatia's Ban Jelačić, told the people of Boka to support Jelačić and warned them against reintroducing Venetian rule—on pain of a Montenegrin invasion.

All Europe was in chaos, including the Adriatic coast. Montengrins, secretly and without the bishop's authorization, came to the aid of the Grbljani, who were no more willing to pay their taxes to Austria than they had been to pay them to the Turks. The bishop also offered help to the Serbs in Vojvodina and even to the Russian Czar. He was not satisfied with the outcome of the Balkan conflicts and said it would have been better if an expedition against Bosnia had been mounted. He was, from first to last, both the ruler of Montenegro and a Serbian patriot.

Gravely ill from the tuberculosis that would kill him, Njegoš lived out his last days trying to solve a dispute with Austria over munitions imports and working on a reconciliation between Patriarch Rajačić and Bishop Atanacković. In a vain attempt to recover his failing health, the vladika went to Naples, where Ljubomir Nenadović visited him in 1851. When an English lord, who much admired the bishop, asked him to inscribe his picture with two or three lines of verse, Njegoš simply signed his name and returned the picture, saying:

My verses are all sad, and I write no more of them. Before me I see a grave stone on which is inscribed: "Here lies the bishop of Montenegro. He is dead and did not live to see the salvation of his people." And when you see this picture, remember the millions of Christians who are my brothers, and who, without any rights, are groaning under the inhuman hands of the Turks. When you go to London, and when you show this picture to your friends, do not say to them: "This is the ruler of a fortunate people." Tell them, "The Serbs could defeat the Turks, but they cannot arouse pity in you Christians."[6]

Njegoš died shortly thereafter (on October 19, 1851), still brooding on the sufferings of the Serbian people. On his last day, he received Communion and commended his soul and the poor people of Montenegro to the Lord. In his last will and testament, Njegoš designated as his successor his nephew Danilo, who at the time of the bishop's death was in Vienna. His absence of two months from Cetinje made it easy for the bishop's brother Pero, president of the Senate and one of the richest and most prominent men in Montenegro, to create a faction among the headmen to support his own claim to power. However, the fact that Danilo was the legitimate successor and that he enjoyed Russia's support seems to have been decisive for him to be confirmed as Montenegro's supreme ruler at the headmen's assembly in January 1852.

In March of the same year, the Senate decided to reestablish the Montenegrin state as a secular principality, reserving to the bishop responsibility for the Church. Perhaps the time had come in Montenegro for a separation of the clerical and secular powers, but the vladika's nephew was also rumored to have fallen in love with a beautiful woman he was determined to make his wife. Danilo traveled to Russia to secure Czar Nicholas' approval of the new arrangement and ratification of his title. The young (he was 25 at his accession) but determined Prince Danilo skillfully consolidated his position, and his chief political opponents emigrated in November of 1853.

A Secular Principality

Throughout his brief reign, Prince Danilo worked tirelessly to achieve his objectives. He wanted to secure, above all, international recognition of Montenegrin independence, but he also aimed at modernizing and

Prince Danilo Petrović

consolidating his infant state and turning the hereditary prince into an absolute monarch. His General National Code, promulgated at the assembly of headmen and chieftains at Cetinje in 1855, went a long way toward accomplishing his goals. In its 95 articles, the code abolished the old patriarchal way of life and the autonomy of the clans. While assuring equality under the law, the Code of Danilo also regulated the entire social, economic, and political life of the country. Montenegrins, as Danilo must have known, would not surrender their independent way of life without a fight, but the four uprisings that broke out—in the Piperi (1852), the Bjelopavlići (1854), and the Kuči (1855 and 1856)—were all ruthlessly put down. The Kuči paid the highest price: About 200 people, children among them, were murdered, 13 villages were torched, 800 homes were plundered, and 1,000 head of cattle and 3,000 other domestic animals were seized. It is perhaps no accident that the clans of the Brda would be more inclined, in future years, to favor union with Serbia and an end to the Petrović dynasty.

Order could not have been effectively maintained, if Prince Danilo had not reorganized the army and increased the number and authority of the *Perjanici* (plume-helmeted police). As early as 1853, he had organized a "cross-bearing army" of nearly 10,000 men, divided into units of 10, 100, and 1,000 soldiers, with names (*e.g.*, decuries and centuries) reminiscent of ancient Rome. The soldiers were not well equipped, but Danilo did introduce the first artillery into the army. The Perjanici, increased to 70, were given additional authority to crack down on bribery and corruption.

Danilo was grimly determined to impose order on his rough people and to eliminate opposition. Njegoš had been content with declaring Marko Djilas an outlaw, but the famous hajduk's existence must have seemed like a thorn in his side, and Marko was lured out of his cave on a pledge of truce and gunned down by a party led by the district captain, Akica Ćorović, who jammed his rifle butt into the outlaw's mouth when he tried to utter some dying words (probably a curse).

Danilo took a firm position on taxes, and during his reign there were no recorded cases of tax evasion. Article 59 of his code stipulated that Montenegrins were obligated to pay "a tribute now and forever in the future, which the local chieftains and headmen shall collect and in the national coffers at the appointed day each year deposit." Tax evasion was not to be treated as a misdemeanor: The offender was to be punished as a "traitor and enemy of our nation." An independent Montenegrin state required a regular tax income, but Danilo was also aware of the need to protect the fledgling economy from Austria. He instituted a tariff on Austrian goods, which were imported from the coastal towns, and he farmed out the customs service to headmen, from which the state derived income as well as the basis of a bureaucracy.

Before he had completed the first year of his reign, Prince Danilo faced the first of a series of Turkish invasions. The ruler of Bosnia and Hercegovina, Omer-pasha Latas, organized an expedition to punish the Montenegrins for aiding the Serbs—Muslim as well as Christian—in Hercegovina and to put an end to the guerilla raids. Omer-pasha had been careful to lure the still-resentful Piperi to his side. Prince Danilo called for a general mobilization and raised an army of 3,000 to 4,000 men to face an invasion force of over 20,000 Muslims. The Montenegrins (not just men but women also) were fierce in defending their land, but they were unable to halt the invading army.

This was no mere raid for the sake of plunder or revenge. Omer-pasha was apparently pursuing the traditional strategy and aiming to detach the Brda from Montenegro as the first step toward subduing the whole of Montenegro. Danilo, however, made an appeal to Russia and Austria, and the mere threat of their intervention was enough to alarm the sultan, who ordered Omer-pasha to abandon his campaign.

In reorganizing his state and defending it from the Turks, Danilo had paved the way for international recognition of Montenegro as a sovereign state. He had hoped for Russia to take the lead, but he was disappointed. In March 1856, when the Turkish representative to a conference in Paris observed that there was nothing to be said of Montenegro except "that it is part of the Turkish Empire," the Russian delegate made no objection. Danilo gave up on the Russians and turned to France as a potential protector of Montenegrin independence. He also sent a diplomatic protest to European capitals, declaring that the Turks had never, in fact, ruled Montenegro and asking for recognition of his country's independence and its rights to the parts of Hercegovina and Albania that had once belonged to Zeta. When Danilo arrived in Paris (in 1857) to advance his claims in person, the government of Napoleon III, while it made lavish expressions of its goodwill and support, refused to accede to the prince's request for an independent status.

Danilo, in his quest for international recognition, faced almost insurmountable obstacles, and he wisely concentrated his efforts on a more realistic goal: to normalize the border with the Ottoman Empire, as Njegoš had established the Austrian frontier. The 1850's were troubled waters for Danilo's fishing expeditions. The Crimean War between Russia and Turkey (with the Turks' British allies) offered a tempting opportunity for Montenegro. Austria, however, was firmly opposed to any Montenegrin move that would help, however indirectly, the Russians.

Closer to home, Serbs in Hercegovina were engaged in a struggle for their independence from the Turks, who had stepped up their persecution of Christians. Danilo's decision to support his brother Serbs and their leader, Vojvoda Luka Vukalović, led inevitably to war with Turkey. Turkish raids inflicted a great deal of damage and suffering, but overall it was not much of a war. The one real battle was fought in 1858 at Grahovo, where the Montenegrins and Hercegovinians scored a brilliant victory over the Turks, whom they pursued all the way to Trebinje.

The Montenegrins were under the command of Mirko Petrović, whom his brother Prince Danilo elevated to grand duke. However, they were unable to reap the rewards of their success when France, Russia, and Austria intervened and set up a border commission, which acknowledged the sultan's sovereign authority over Montenegro but, at the same time, increased Montenegro's actual territory in Brda and Hercegovina. Montenegrins, despite their failure to hold on to all their conquered territory, could take comfort from the fact that they now had, for the first time, official state borders.

Even without international recognition of Montenegrin sovereignty, Danilo's achievement was historic, but he was not to enjoy the savor of victory for long. The prince was murdered in Kotor on August 12, 1860.

It is not known whether the assassin was hired by personal enemies or domestic political opponents.

Notes

For the period from the election of Petar I to the death of Prince Danilo, I have continued to follow Popović, Gopčević, and Medaković among the older historians as well as the straightforward account more recently provided by Sima Ćirković.

1. Gopčević, pp. 240-41.

2. Boehm, p. 59.

3. *Mémoire du Marechal Duc de Raguse*, (Paris, 1858) II. P.108.

4. Popović, pp. 172 ff.

5. M. Djilas, *Land Without Justice*, pp. 8-12.

6. Cf. Nenadović, *Pisma*.

THE LONG REIGN OF
MONTENEGRO S ONLY KING

Prince Danilo had only one child, a daughter, and on departing for Paris in 1857, he had named his 18-year-old nephew Nikola as his successor. The young Nikola's succession could not be challenged, because his father Mirko, who provided invaluable support in the early years of his reign, was already the most influential man in Montenegro. In his long reign, Nikola would face an apparently endless series of crises, both foreign and domestic, and although he was to prove himself to be a harsh and autocratic ruler, Nikola was (like his father and uncle) the kind of strong man Montenegro needed at the helm if it were to weather the storms.

Although Prince Nikola inherited a country that was enjoying a rare period of domestic tranquility, he had hardly taken his place on the throne when he was drawn into supporting the insurgency in Hercegovina, led by Luka Vukalović. The Serbs' main grievances had to do with excessive and capricious taxation. To deal with the agrarian unrest, the Turks unleashed the worst elements in Hercegovina: irregular bands of Muslim fanatics that gloried in the violent persecution of Christians. Although Serbia, because of its status within the Ottoman Empire, was in no position to provide assistance, the Hercegovinians had been impressed by the Montenegrin victory at Grahovo, and they succeeded in persuading Prince Nikola's government to assist them, more or less openly.

The prince's father, Mirko, thought the time had come to expel the Turks from Hercegovina. The European powers were of a different opinion. After defeating Russia in the Crimean War, Austria and Britain were determined to prop up the ailing Ottoman Empire. Vienna and Istanbul appear to have come to an agreement, and the British ambassador to Turkey, Sir Henry Bulwer, blamed all the disturbances on Montenegro. Prince Nikola responded by sending a circular letter around the European capitals, describing the atrocities committed by the Turks. A European commission sent to investigate and mediate the disputes, though the members were divided, worked to end the rebellion on terms that were less favorable than the Turks themselves had granted only five years earlier.

By the time of Danilo's assassination in 1860, relations between Turkey and Montenegro had reached the critical point. The Turks declared war in April 1862. Omer-pasha attacked with an army of 29,000 men, which was subsequently increased to 55,000. Montenegrin and Hercegovinian forces, which numbered approximately 15,000, dug in their heels in the Duga Gorge and at Medun, but they were not strong enough to block the Turkish advance. The Turks, hoping to dampen Montenegrin enthusiasm for war, made peace overtures and promised to respect the rights of the Serbs. The effect was spoiled by the Muslims' renewed attacks, in which women, old men, and children were slaughtered.

The Serb leadership, was unfortunately, divided. Luka Vukalović had alarmed Vojvoda Mirko by entering into direct contact with Ilija Garašanin, prime minister of Serbia, and Vukalović was stripped of his position in the Montenegrin army in a manner that was calculated to insult the Hercegovinian's pride. The Turks exploited the differences in the leadership, but they grew increasingly fearful of Russian intervention.

Luka Vukalović, despite his quarrel with Duke Mirko, did gain an unusual ally: Don Ivan Musić, a Catholic priest, who led 400 Catholics to fight on the Serbian side. Catholic Austria, which had apparently come to an understanding with the sultan, was far from helpful, and the Austrian army seized Serbian trenches and guns and indirectly aided the Turks whenever they could. There was no peace, either, in eastern Montenegro, where the Vasojevići were attacked by Turks from Kolašin. The Turks continued to bring in fresh troops, especially Albanians, and the continuous fighting reduced the Montenegrin army to the point that it might not have held Cetinje if Russia had not interceded with Constantinople. Under the peace treaty, signed in September 1862, Montenegro did not give up any territory but it did have to promise not to support insurgents.[1]

The failures of 1862 taught the Montenegrins a valuable lesson: The army had to be strengthened. With Serbia's help, domestic arms production was increased, and Montenegro also received 5,000 rifles, one battery of mountain cannon, and a quantity of ammunition. Serbian officers arrived to train Montenegrin troops (whose strength was brought up to 17,000) and undertake the reform of the army. Confident in her remodeled army and invigorated by financial help from Russia and Serbia, Montenegro bravely stepped up to face the "Eastern Crisis" and to play a far from insignificant role in the war of 1876-78.

The broader struggle was once again triggered by an uprising of Serbs in Bosnia and Hercegovina. Serbia and Montenegro supported the rebellion, both overtly and covertly, and jointly declared war on Turkey in June 1876. In August, Montenegrin forces handed the Turkish army stunning defeats at Fundina and Vučji Do, while in the east, the Vasojević insurgents were also celebrating successes. A truce was negotiated on November 1, 1876 with Russia's mediation, and continued until April 24, 1877, when Russia declared war on Turkey. Montenegro did the same two days later.

Russia seemed eager to enter the fray. The defeat in the Crimean War 20 years earlier, coupled with demands for reforming Russia on a Western model, had convinced Czar Alexander II of the need to curry favor with the European powers and to maintain good relations with Turkey. A nationalist uprising in Poland, however, and mounting pressure within Russia to help Orthodox Serbs set the czar on a collision course with the Ottoman Empire. In 1865, he had encouraged an uprising on Crete, and in 1870 he had helped the Bulgars to establish an autocephalous church. Turkey's criminal behavior toward Bosnian Serbs and Bulgars (the "Bulgarian atrocities") produced a wave of popular hostility toward Turkey throughout Europe, which the Russians hoped to turn to their own advantage. In England, the wily Prime Minister Benjamin Disraeli was adamantly opposed to Russian ambitions, but his great Liberal rival William Gladstone thundered out, in a pamphlet that reached tens of thousands of Englishmen, that the Turks had to be thrown out "bag and baggage . . . from the provinces they have desolated and profaned."[2] It was Gladstone who encouraged Tennyson to be the Byron of Montenegro and wrote an essay to accompany his sonnet.

The Russians quickly invaded Bulgaria and besieged the Turkish fortress of Pleven. Osman-pasha, the Turkish commander of the 40,000-man garrison, was forced to surrender. Meanwhile, troops from Serbia, which moved south to support the Russians, took key points in Old Serbia: Niš, Pirot, and Vranje. Many Serbian volunteers from Austria-Hungary and the Ottoman Empire took part in the war, especially in southeastern Serbia. Serbia succeeded in almost doubling its territory. Although its army reached Kosovo Polje, the peace negotiations forced it to withdraw.

In Montenegro the Turkish army (numbering some 65,000) attacked from three directions: from Gacko, Berane, and Podgorica, hoping to reach Cetinje by passing through the territory of the Bjelopavlići. Heavy battles were fought in the Ostrog Gorge and at the Morača Monastery. In the end, Montenegro succeeded in liberating much of Hercegovina. When the Turkish army in Bulgaria suffered defeats at the hands of the Russians, the Montenegrins were able to take Bar and Ulcinj as well as several forts on Lake Scutari. In the Treaty of San Stefano, signed in March 1878, Turkey finally recognized Montenegro's independence, but the terms of the treaty alarmed the Great Powers, which regarded Turkey, even in decline, as the policeman in the Balkans and an obstacle to Russian expansion. One large sticking point was the creation, under Russian protection, of a large Bulgarian principality, which encroached upon Serbian national interests in Old Serbia and Macedonia.

Austrian Emperor Franz Josef was dismayed to see this eruption of Slavic nationalism on his very doorstep, and British Prime Minister Disraeli was equally unhappy with the success of Russia, England's antagonist in the Crimean War. When German Chancellor Bismarck agreed to play the role of "honest broker" and proposed a meeting in Berlin, the czar agreed: He could not risk conflict with all the European powers at the same time. At the Congress of Berlin, held a few months later in July to revise the treaty, Montenegro, although robbed of many of the fruits of victory, achieved fully independent status and acquired extensive territorial gains, going from 4,000 to nearly 10,000 square kilometers and gaining the important towns of Nikšić, Kolašin, Spuž, Podgorica, Žabljak, Bar, and Ulcinj. The acquisition of a coastline was of vast economic and cultural significance. Montenegro would no longer be a confederation of landlocked mountain tribes but an independent state meeting the entire world on the shores of the Adriatic.

Serbia and Montenegro scored another victory at Berlin, when the territory of the proposed Bulgarian state was reduced. Unfortunately, this also had the effect of restricting Russia's influence in the Balkans to the benefit of Austria-Hungary, which was allowed to occupy Bosnia-Hercegovina. Despite their military successes, Serbs now faced an ambitious Hapsburg neighbor to the west and had to relinquish Old Serbia and Macedonia to the Ottoman Empire. Austria, which now controlled the strip of Raška separating Serbia from Montenegro, was in a position to play even more dangerous games in the Balkans. Serbia had to pay a high price for Austrian support in Berlin, and the Serbian economy was soon made highly dependent on that of Austria-Hungary.

Under the treaty of Berlin, Montenegro also found itself squeezed by Austria-Hungary. Although Montenegrins had secured vital access to the sea at Bar and Ulcinj, there were significant restrictions. Montenegro was forbidden to develop a navy, and had to accept the same maritime law that applied to Dalmatia. Austria now had the authority to supervise the entire Montenegrin seacoast. Those restrictions were only abolished in 1909.

Russia was of little help to Montenegro in its diplomatic struggle with Austria-Hungary. Absorbed in its internal problems and by its struggle with Japan, Russia came to an agreement with Austria to accept the *status quo* and to acquiesce in the expansion of Austrian and German influence in the Balkans, where German princelings were set up as kings in Bulgaria, Greece, and Rumania. Even in Serbia, King Milan Obrenović was content to allow his country to become political satellite of Vienna.

Austria Sows Discord

Austria was far from content with its economic and political domination in the Balkans, and its statesmen were ever on the lookout for new methods of applying the traditional strategy of "divide and rule." The most productive tactic was the invention of new ethnic identities, which could be used to drive a wedge into the fissures that erupt even within the most unified nations. Count Benjamin von Kallay, an Hungarian diplomat and historian, was the master of this strategy. As ambassador to Belgrade (1868-75), viceroy in Bosnia (1882-1903), and author of a *History of the Serbs*, Kallay became the Dual Monarchy's point man on the Balkans.

Kallay's masterpiece of strategic deception was the creation of an independent Bosnian language, culture, and nation, to which he applied the term "Bosniaks." A vital part of the ploy was the Bogomil theory of Bosnian Muslim identity, a fraud that still catches unwary Western writers. According to Kallay, modern Bosnian Muslims are descended from a distinctive nation with a unique culture; these Bosniaks had adhered to the Bogomil sect, and, persecuted by Orthodox and Catholic churches, they opted for Islam as a means of preserving their cultural identity. To reinforce his theories, Kallay banned the importation of Serbian books and newspapers into Bosnia and even put his own book on the index, because it gave the Serbs too favorable treatment.

Kallay also promoted "Macedonianism," even as he was encouraging the two Serbian states to expand into Macedonia (rather than into

Hungarian-held Vojvodina), and he and other Austro-Hungarian diplomats, though ever alert to denounce the crimes of Serbs and Bulgars, conveniently turned a blind eye to the atrocities committed by Albanians in Kosovo and Macedonia.

Benevolent Despotism

As an internationally recognized state, that had to conduct relations with foreign governments, Montenegro had to convert its miniscule foreign service, which had been established as an office of the Senate only four years before the Congress of Berlin, into a foreign ministry. All real authority, however, remained in the hands of the prince. Montenegro now established relations with all the major powers except Germany, but it maintained permanent diplomatic missions only in Turkey, Serbia, France, and (for a few months in 1918) the United States, in addition to consulates in Rome, Trieste, and Kotor. Eleven countries (but not Germany) had diplomatic missions at Cetinje, and three kept consulates at Bar and Podgorica.

The delay in establishing relations with Germany was accidental. When Baron Testa, who had been appointed "rapporteur" of the Protocol on Montenegro, arrived in Cetinje in 1879, he spent three days without being received by any official. Prince Nikola, along with Foreign Minister Stanko Radonjić, was traveling in the hinterland, and no one in Cetinje was willing to meet an important foreign official without Prince Nikola's blessing. An exasperated Testa finally went to Kotor, from which he sent Bismarck a telegram describing his futile mission. The Chancellor, characterizing the incident as *"ein unglaublich Skandal,"* sent a circular to all German diplomatic missions, declaring that "Montenegro is to be ignored as if it did not exist."

Although Montenegro had secured its independence, the situation was far from stable. The people were still very poor, though some land became available as many Turks and other Muslims, refusing to live under a Christian government, fled the country. Prince Nikola appropriated large chunks of land for himself, his friends, and relations, but many peasants were also able to acquire property, and the feudal system of the Turks gave way to a system of peasant freeholds. Nonetheless, large numbers of Montenegrins continued to emigrate in search of economic opportunities—48,000 left between 1879 and 1892. About 20,000 of them went to Serbia, but many others made their way to America.

Following in the footsteps of his predecessor, Prince Nikola centralized the Montenegrin political system. He not only replaced the Senate with a State Council and a High Court but he also divided the country into five administrative districts, each one reporting directly to the interior minister (who was answerable to the king). The districts were themselves divided into captaincies (56 in 1904), which corresponded to tribal territories. The corruption and capriciousness of the untrained and poorly paid administrators did little to reconcile the people to the growing power of the state.

Nikola's state was a strange hybrid that could use bureaucratic officials to carry out an act of blood revenge. When Akica Ćorović came upon Marko Djilas's nephew Aleksa, several years after Marko had been killed, he taunted the boy, who went home and asked for a gun to shoot wolves. He quickly intercepted the captain and blew away his chest. Aleksa Djilas fled immediately to Nikšić, which was still in Turkish hands, but the order went out from Cetinje to exterminate the entire clan. Prince Nikola assigned the task to his own father-in-law, who arranged a humiliating death for the youth. Aleksa's godfather, who was in on the plot, invited him to a party, and while he was enjoying the hospitality, he was struck on the head with a wooden mallet—killed, in other words— like an animal. For the officials in Cetinje, commented Aleksa's grandson Milovan Djilas, "not even spiritual kinship was sacred"—a strange complaint from a leader of the Montenegrin communists who slaughtered their own relatives and employed, on at least one occasion, the very same instrument of death as the murderers of Aleksa Djilas.

Although Djilas described Nikola as more sly than bold, the king followed up the murder by sending an attack meant to wipe out the entire Djilas brotherhood. Of the males, only Aleksa's infant son was spared.[3]

Such incidents did not endear the Prince to the people of the Brda, but he was, nonetheless, a ruler to respect. Nikola's success in defending the Montenegro and expanding its territory enhanced his prestige and encouraged him to regard Montenegro as his personal property—an attitude that was often resented by more than a few of the headmen, who were, however, never strong enough to form a faction to oppose the prince. Opposition was to come only in the early 20th century, when Montenegrin students educated in Belgrade, where they absorbed radical ideas, injected a more Western and "progressive" vision into Montenegro. Modernization, however, is a complex business. Movements that begin by calling for reform of the political system all too often end up destroying the national heart and soul, and this charge can certainly be laid at the door of the radical (especially Marxist) intellectuals who were to play so large a role in Montenegro and Yugoslavia throughout the 20th century.

Facing domestic and international disapproval of his patriarchal regime, Prince Nikola promulgated a constitution in December 1905. In this, too, he acted as an autocrat, giving the National Assembly no opportunity to debate or emend the draft document. Montenegro was made a constitutional monarchy, whose hereditary ruler was sacrosanct and accountable to no one. Not content with exercising a monopoly on executive power, the prince shared legislative power with the National Assembly and served as supreme commander of the army, with the right to declare war and enter into alliances with other states. He also appointed state officials, convened the National Assembly, and—though the courts were declared independent—directly selected the judges.

Montenegro's first political party, the National Party, grew out of a club whose members were younger and educated deputies who adopted the program of Serbia's Radical Party. The "Clubmen," (or *klubaši*), as they were known, professed themselves loyal to the prince and to monarchy, but the ever- suspicious Nikola decided to create a "True National Party" (*pravaši* or "True Blues") as a conservative counterweight. Nikola's most severe critics were young Montenegrins in Belgrade, who formed the Club of University Youth. In 1907, the students issued a proclamation of the "Serbian Youth from Montenegro." To the prince's ears, it sounded like the opening shot of a revolution. He accused the National Party of complicity and undertook a systematic persecution of its members. The National Party did not resist the crackdown and decided against running candidates in the next elections. Several members wisely chose to emigrate.

Although the National Party had been permanently eliminated from the political scene, Nikola was not satisfied. He organized a political trial of his opponents, and with the evidence of 15 grenades sent to Cetinje by Montenegrin students in Belgrade, he charged the "bombers" (that is, even his mildest critics) with conspiring against the prince, his home, and the state. The 132 defendants were sentenced to death or imprisonment. Even Nikola's conservative former prime minister, Andrija Radović, received a 15-year sentence. Although the death sentences were commuted, the trial succeeded only in creating a bad impression, especially among Radović's clan, the Bjelopavlići.

Isolated from criticism, the prince staged another political trial in which 161 members of the National Party were accused of "treason and conspiracy to over-throw the government of Montenegro." The closed-door proceedings, conducted by the Grand Military Tribunal in Kolašin, resulted in 59 prison sentences and five executions. In August 1910 the prince celebrated the 50th anniversary of his reign by crowning himself king and proclaiming Montenegro a kingdom.

Relations with Austria and Serbia

The elevation of Montenegro to a kingdom could not have been managed without Austrian support. This new cordiality between the Austrian eagle and the Montenegrin falcon was a marked improvement over the tense relations of preceding years. Austria's decision to annex Bosnia-Hercegovina in 1908 had angered Serbs everywhere and encouraged Prince Nikola to make up the quarrel with his son-in-law, King Petar of Serbia. Nikola strongly resented Serbia's growing wealth and prestige, and he was convinced that the Serbian government, perhaps the king himself, was behind the conspiracies that were being hatched by the Belgrade students.

Despite the growing perception that a union of all Serbian peoples was inevitable, Prince Nikola insisted upon Montenegro's tradition of "eternal" independence and repeated the old sayings that Montenegrins were the "best Serbs." This chauvinism was partly the instinctive reflex of a Romantic nationalist and partly a calculated policy to treat Montenegro as the Serbian Piedmont, the little country around which a great Serbia could be constructed. Nikola's chauvinism exacerbated his already poor relations with the kings of Serbia, whom he regarded as upstarts and obstacles to his dynastic ambitions. Although the Petrović dynasty entered somewhat late into the game of European royalty, Prince Nikola had made excellent dynastic moves, giving two daughters to cousins of the emperor of Russia, one to Petar Karadjordjević (later King Petar I of Serbia), and another, Jelena, to the heir to the Italian throne.

During the crisis over the annexation of Bosnia, relations had warmed between Montenegro and Serbia, despite the failure of either to gain allies that would make resistance to Austrian aggression a viable possibility. Unfortunately, just as it began to look as if the two countries might display a united front to Austria-Hungary, an abortive uprising broke out in Kolašin, and harsh sentences were meted out, not just to the conspirators themselves but to the pro-Serbian *klubaši*. Montenegro's official press launched a vicious attack on Serbia's Prime Minister Nikola Pašić, and Prince Nikola and his sons flew into Austria's waiting arms. Mirko, the Prince's second son, told the Austrian ambassador, "Montenegrins are not Serbians . . . We do not want anything to do with Serbia."[4] Although Mirko's declaration did not amount to a repudiation of his Serbian heritage ("Serbian" in this context means Serbs from Serbia), it did show how far Nikola's government was willing to go in distancing Montenegrins from their cousins. In this new atmosphere, the Austrian foreign ministry and the emperor himself were all too happy to drive another wedge into Serbian unity by stroking the prince's vanity, and Austria officially congratulated King Nikola, in August 1910, on his new rank.

Balkan Wars

The Balkan states, some of them still fresh with the dew of their recent creation, were eager to find an opportunity of expanding their territory and pushing the Turks, finally, out of Europe. They had an unexpected ally in the Young Turks, who came to power in 1908 on the promise of modernizing the Turkish state. The Young Turks were determined to impose the Turkish language and culture on their dwindling dominions and their high-handed ways brought a new wave of uprisings and European outrage. Harold Temperley, who was in the Balkans at the time, remarked that "the Young Turk and the Old Tyrant were not very different in aim, however much they differed in name," and he himself witnessed what happened when a Bulgarian in Macedonia fled to the hills to avoid paying taxes: "The Turkish soldiers descended on his house, set it on fire, and drove his family out on the hillside."[5]

The test of the Young Turks' policies came in Albania, where the Catholics in particular were determined to maintain their identity and religion. In despair, the Malissori turned for help to their traditional enemy, Orthodox Montenegro. King Nikola had to walk cautiously, assuring his Austrian and Russian friends that he was not stirring up a Balkan war, while at the same time offering refuge and support to Albanian Catholic rebels who made Podgorica their capital.[6]

Although Nikola had quite definite ambitions to rule over at least part of Albania, that was only a part of the Serbian dream. Serbian Christians in Kosovo and Macedonia were still subject to a Turkish regime that, in changing its form from monarchy to oligarchy, was doing little to improve the lot of its Christian subjects. Despite the jealousies and suspicions that had plagued their relations, Serbia and Montenegro were able to come to terms, first separately with Bulgaria and Greece and then with each other, for a joint effort against Turkey. The time was ripe for a renewal of the struggle. In Libya, Turkey was embroiled in a conflict with Italy; the Albanians had begun a struggle for national liberation; in Turkey itself the regime of the Young Turks was plagued by mutinies.

The First Balkan War was the fulfillment of a longstanding dream. Montenegro and Serbia, acting in concert with Russia, had already liberated many Christians from the Turkish yoke. The final push began in 1912, when the Christian states in the Balkans (Serbia, Montenegro, Bulgaria, and Greece) formed an alliance whose object was the liberation of all Balkan Christians from Ottoman rule. Although the European powers

King Nikola Petrović

warned Balkan states against the war they were contemplating, Turkish attacks on Christians in Macedonia gave them the excuse they needed. The Christian allies scored major victories on all fronts—in Kosovo, Macedonia, and the Aegean.

The Montenegrin army, though a poorly equipped militia organized on a territorial (and thus tribal) basis, fought bravely, its losses amounting to 9,500 dead and wounded. Montenegrin forces collaborated with the Serbian army in the regions of Raska, Kosovo, and Metohija, but one of the king's main ob-

Serbian and Montenegrin soldiers in liberated Metohija, 1912

jectives (as it always had been) was the occupation of Scutari. Here, he was less successful. Montenegrin forces made little headway toward capturing the town, and though they were cheered by the arrival of 30,000 soldiers from Serbia, they could not mount the final attack because of intervention by the Great Powers, who protested the siege of Scutari and sent eight warships into Montenegrin waters. Russia exerted pressure from the other direction, forcing Serbia to withdraw its army from Scutari. In defiance, King Nikola and his high command used their artillery to bring the city to its knees, and Montenegrin troops marched into Scutari. By the Treaty of London, signed in May 1913, Turkey lost its last foothold in Europe.

The Montegrin victory only stiffened the Great powers' resolve to defend Turkish rule, and King Nikola, unable to risk going to war with the greatest states in Europe, told Edward Grey, the English foreign minister, that while Montenegrin self-respect did not permit him to give into pressure, he did agree to entrust the fate of Scutari to the European powers. Austria-Hungary took the lead in promoting a greater Albanian state, and although the final results were less grandiose than what was initially proposed, Montenegro was deprived of the plain of Scutari, where the Balšići had once ruled.

The victors in the First Balkan War soon fell to quarrelling over the spoils. Bulgaria, though it gained enough territory to arouse the jealousy of its allies, was not content to leave any part of Macedonia in Serbian hands. In the Second Balkan War, which pitted Serbia and Greece against Bulgaria, Montenegro naturally took the side of Serbia, and in July 1913, King Nikola declared war on Bulgaria and sent 13,000 troops to Macedonia, telling the soldiers he expected them to do their duty in the "defense of our Serbian interests." It was during these Balkan Wars that King Nikola displayed both the courage and the pan-Serbian patriotism that were the best justifications of his authoritarian regime. The Serbian-Greek alliance, supported by Rumania, administered a complete thrashing to Bulgaria in a campaign along the Bregalnica river. Montenegro, which had sent the "Dečani" detachment of 13,000 men, did well out of the war, increasing its territory by 5,000 square kilometers (including a part of Lake Scutari), to encompass over 14,442 square kilometers.

Serbia and Montenegro emerged victorious and strengthened from the Balkan Wars. They had nearly doubled their territories and now faced each other across a common border. On both sides of the friendly frontier, it was commonly taken for granted that the two states would take the necessary steps toward union and for the eventual liberation of all Serbian areas across the Drina and the Sava. Frustrated in her "divide and rule" policy in the Balkans, Austria-Hungary began to agitate (in alliance with Germany) for war against Serbia as the most effective means of preventing the emergence of a strong Serbian state. The assassination of Archduke Franz Ferdinand in Sarajevo, which was the bitter fruit of Austria's annexation of Bosnia, provided the convenient pretext for aggression, but it was not the actual cause of the Great War. European nations had been constantly at war since Italy and Turkey clashed in North Africa, and every government that would participate in the conflagration of World War I had its war plans drawn up years in advance.

World War I

Throughout the war, Serbia and Montenegro fought together as closely coordinated allies. At the beginning of the war, Montenegrin forces were in charge of defending the upper Drina as well as organizing the offensive in eastern Bosnia. Even in this atmosphere of patriotic cooperation, there were tensions when, in June 1915, Nikola insisted on occupying Scutari against the wishes of General Janković, head of the Serbian Military Mission in Montenegro. Janković's successor, by concentrating forces in the Sanjak and Hercegovina, left Kotor exposed to an Austrian attack. Relations deteriorated between the King Nikola and Serbian Prime Minister Pašić, who was already working with the former Montenegrin prime minister, Andrija Radović, to arrange a postwar unification of the two Serb states.

Later in 1915, when Serbia, attacked by Austria-Hungary, Germany, and Bulgaria and left without allied support, was forced to withdraw its government and army to Corfu, Montenegro defended the Serbian troops that were retreating across its territory. In spite of the heroic defense along the Drina and the Lim rivers, and especially at Mojkovac, Montenegro was driven off the field by the powerful Austro-Hungarian and German armies.

Mojkovac was the last great battle fought by the forces of independent Montenegro, but it was fought after the king's surrender. The Montenegrin army was disbanded, and King Nikola and his government went into exile. Djilas, whose home was near the battle, reflected later in his book *Land Without Justice*: "A whole people—the Montenegrin—which understood life in terms of war and glory, stopped fighting. A people's army and a state had ceased to be." Pašić, his eyes already fixed on a postwar union, refused to deal with the Montenegrin government in exile.

The government of Serbia, despite the military disasters it had suffered, eventually rallied to preserve its nationhood. On Corfu, despite the terrible losses they had sustained on the retreat, Serbs succeeded in keeping the main forces of their army intact. The army was eventually transported to the Salonika front, where its numbers were increased by Serbian volunteers. After breaking through the front in September 1918, the Serbian army went on to liberate Serbia, Vojvodina, and Montenegro. Bosnia-Hercegovina, Dalmatia, Croatia and Slovenia were soon freed from Austro-Hungarian troops, and backed by the victorious allies, Serbia realized the long-held dream of a common Serbian state, but this dream was swiftly exchanged for another dream (which turned out to be a nightmare) of a Union of Southern Slavs.

Throughout the war, however, King Nikola and his supporters had favored a concept of union that would preserve the integrity of the Montenegrin state and the honor of the Petrović family by making Montenegro a sort of Bavaria within a greater Serbia. Nikola's surrender and flight rendered this option impossible. Nikola Pašić persuaded his ally Radović to submit a formal memorandum to King Nikola, urging his abdication for the sake of union with Serbia and, ultimately, with other South Slav peoples. Prince Regent Aleksandar would succeed to the rule of both kingdoms, but his successor would be Aleksandar's cousin Danilo, King Nikola's elder son. Nikola was at first inclined to accept the offer (or at least said he was), but after spending time with his daughter, the queen of Italy, he changed his mind. The Italians, who dreamed of succeeding to Venice's position as Queen of the Adriatic, obviously preferred to keep the Serbs divided and weak. Nikola's intrigues, far from helping his cause, served to disgust many Montenegrins.

Events moved swiftly. Andrija Radović agreed to head up the Montenegrin Committee for the Union of Montenegro and Serbia, which had been formed in Geneva and quickly aroused enthusiasm among Montenegrins. The popular appeal of the unification movement can be measured by the number of Montenegrin volunteers they succeeded in recruiting for the Serbian army. The committee had to move quickly to unify Serbia and Montenegro unconditionally *before* the Serbs were merged into a South Slavic state. The future of a united Serbia, they believed, should not be dependent upon the ideas and aspirations of anyone else, neither the victorious allies nor the Slavic peoples being liberated from Hapsburg control.

The Montenegrin Committee, like similar groups in Vojvodina, Bosnia, Hercegovina, Dalmatia (and throughout the Hapsburg dominions in Central and Eastern Europe), believed in the principles of national self-determination and representative democracy that were so loudly proclaimed by Britain and the United States. As the Serbian troops were liberating the lands of the Southern Slavs, the Montenegrin Committee was preparing the way for a meeting of democratically elected representatives in Podgorica to settle the question definitively. Supporters of a unified Serbia also set up a temporary executive central committee, and—as the Austrian army withdrew—established a local government in every community. It was decided that elections for representatives at the forthcoming Great National Assembly in Podgorica were to be held "under neither Serbian nor Montenegrin electoral law" but according to new regulations designed to ensure fair and free elections. At the beginning of October 1918, members of the Temporary Executive Central Committee arrived in Montenegro, and elections for the representatives took place between November 6-19, 1918.

During the pre-election campaign, King Nikola's followers, who were opposed to the union and were financially supported by Italy, were working active. In Cetinje, two slates of candidates were put forward:

those who supported the union with Serbia and those who opposed it. The two parties were known as the *bjelaši* (Whites) and the *zelenaši* (Greens), named after the colors of their political pamphlets. In many ways, the split between the *bjelaši* and the *zelenaši* was a replay between the *klubaši* and the *pravaši*, with the significant difference that, this time around, the opponents of union with Serbia did not have the state and the police on their side. In the election, the Whites, who were in favor of union, won hands down, and the decision to be made by the Assembly in Podgorica was a foregone conclusion.

At the Assembly, held in Podgorica in November 1918, 176 elected representatives met. In this and similar meetings, the representatives voiced their complaints over King Nikola's nepotism, his despotic treatment of his subjects, and his defeatist conduct in the war. The Assembly received similar complaints from Montenegrin exiles around the world. Montenegrins in America were particularly bitter and warned Nikola's consul-general in New York that he would go to Versailles to plead for the king only at the risk of his own life. Meeting in New York, an assembly of 27 Montenegrin societies in the United States sent a message to Podgorica in which they accused Nikola's government of committing "a crime against Serbdom and its allies, and an unprecedented act of treason in the history of the South Slavs."[8]

Opponents of union, who tried to open a discussion of a more federal solution, were dismissed as irrelevant and reminded of the presence nearby of the Serbian army under the command of Lt. Col. Dušan Simović, an officer trusted by Prince-Regent Aleksandar, who made him royal aide-de-camp. The Italian military, which landed a detachment at Kotor, would have supported the king if Montenegrin volunteers had not forced them to beat a hasty retreat. The Italians left, but they would return 23 years later to take over Montenegro in the name of Nikola's heirs. The king's supporters, including Prime Minister Jovan Plamenac, established contact with Gabriele d'Annunzio, who was launching his filibuster attempt to create a series of five Italian puppet-states along the Adriatic coast, from Montenegro to Fiume (which he succeeded in seizing).

The Assembly, by a vote of 163 members (five members failed to sign, citing reasons of health) declared that "the Serbian people in Montenegro are of one blood, one language, and one aspiration, one religion and custom with the people that live in Serbia and in other Serbian regions." They then proceeded to proclaim the overthrow of King Nikola Petrović and his dynasty, the unification of Serbia and Montenegro under the Karadjordjević dynasty, and the creation of an interim Executive National Committee to govern Montenegro until the union of Montenegro and Serbia was completed. The king and the allies were informed of the decision, and the Executive Committee, once it was elected, confiscated all of the Petrović dynasty's movable property and realestate and forbade King Nikola and his family to return to Montenegro. Montenegro became part of the Kingdom of Serbs, Croats, and Slovenes on December 1, 1918.

Although there was dissension, even among the Orthodox clergy, over the kind of union they wanted with Serbia (depending on whether they adhered to the White or Green factions), there was no dispute over the unity of the Serbian Church. Montenegrin bishops voted unanimously in December on the declaration that "the independent Serbian Orthodox Church in Montenegro unites with the autocephalous Orthodox Church in the Kingdom of Serbia." Autocephaly ("self-headedness") is a very precise term that signifies more than independence. All Orthodox (and Catholic) archbishoprics (metropolitanates) are independent in the sense that they are self-governing. However, an autocephalous church, subject only to the ultimate authority of the ecumenical patriarch in Constantinople, has the power to generate its own bishops and archbishops. This status must be in accordance with the canon law of the Orthodox Church, effected by the ecumenical patriarch, and recognized by other Orthodox Churches.

The Orthodox Church in Montenegro has never, throughout its entire history, been canonically autocephalous. At all times it was the Exarchate of the Holy Serbian Patriarchal Throne of Pec; and it was under the jurisdiction of the Serbian Patriarch, except in those periods when the Patriarchate was abolished by Ottoman decree. Prince-Regent Alexandar's "seizure" of the Montenegrin metropolitanate is purely political propaganda designed to provide a fig leaf of legitimacy to a group of Communists, Muslims, atheists, and defrocked clergymen who started (in the 1990's) to give themselves positions in a nonexistent "Montenegrin Church."

The making of nations is not a clean business, and the losing party had legitimate complaints against the unionists who had ridden roughshod over their opposition. Some Montenegrins, in voting for the White electors, might not have imagined they were voting to eliminate the Montenegrin state entirely. The strong-arm tactics used at the Assembly, combined with the active intervention of Nikola Pašić, were to leave a bad taste in the mouths even of some Montenegrins who actively supported union with Serbia but preferred a traditional marriage to a shotgun wedding. But, if truth be told, the Podgorica Assembly was a more representative and legitimate body than many other congresses that have made nations. It was certainly no less democratic or less legitimate than the similar assemblies that proclaimed the Weimar Republic and Czechoslovakia, and it was far more representative than the assemblies that established the French and American Republics.

The lawyers and troublemakers who overthrew the French monarchy and killed the king and queen may have represented the opinion of Paris and a few other urban centers, but they had to wage a genocidal war against whole regions in order to enforce their new order. Who were the American patriots of 1776 that they had the right to declare independence from Great Britain? Many were distinguished men, but they had won election to the Continental Congress in an atmosphere of intimidation. Most historians would put the level of support for independence at somewhere between a third and a fourth—hardly the electoral base for a country that would pride itself on democracy. And, for that matter, the delegates to the Constitutional Convention, who gathered in Philadelphia in 1787, were authorized only to emend the Articles of Confederation, not to replace them with a new system.

The year 1918 was not a period in history that allowed much time for calm reflection. If Montenegro had kept out of Yugoslavia, there is no doubt what her future would have been: absorption by Italy, whose king was married to Nikola's daughter. In retrospect, it is easy to see that a union of Slavic peoples—Orthodox, Catholic, and Muslims—was not a workable idea. For those who had lived through the exciting wars of liberation and seen the great empires crumble—first the Ottomans and then the Hapsburgs—the important lesson to be drawn was that in unity, there is strength and that division is an open invitation to foreign intervention. This was true in 1918, 1940, 1991, and it is true in 2002.

Notes

Montenegro's participation in the broader Serb struggle against Turkey and Austria is described by Stephenson and by Michael Bora Petrovich. Marriot's classic work on "the Eastern Question" provides an excellent introduction to the Great Power context, and Popović, though an unquestioning supporter of the Petrović dynasty, provides a detailed account of the period through which he lived. For the years leading up to World War I, Treadway has given a masterful analysis.

1. On the war of 1862, see Pavićević, whose work includes a précis in French.

2. *The Bulgarian Horrors and the Question of the East* (London, 1876)

3. Djilas, *Land*, pp. 12-18.

4. Treadway, p. 57.

5. Temperley, p. 322.

6. Treadway, pp. 66-86.

7. National Archives, Washington, D.C. 763.2 189/1860.

MONTENEGRO IN THE FIRST YUGOSLAVIA

With the creation of the Kingdom of Serbs, Croats, and Slovenes, the history of the Montenegrin state comes to an end, to be replaced by the question of the identity and status of Montenegro, a subject that will repeatedly divide the Montenegrins and justify the intervention of foreign powers. Montenegro, at the end of 1918, was in a strange position. Although it was the only component of the new kingdom, apart from Serbia, that had its own experience of statehood, the Montenegrin state ceased to exist, while Croatia, which had surrendered its independence in the 12th century, and Slovenia, which had never been independent, were the constant focus of attention for the Belgrade government, which treated Croat politicians as spokesmen for an ethnic group as well as leaders of political parties.[1] Unlike the states that were cobbled together out of the ruins of Austria-Hungary, Yugoslavia[2] was no mere fiction of the Versailles Treaty. In fact, the allies only grudgingly acknowledged it as a *fait accompli*. Nonetheless, it was doomed to collapse (twice!) of its own contradictions.

Yugoslavism

In retrospect, it is easy to see the dream of a South Slavic state as a delusion that would quickly turn into a nightmare. In the late 19th century, however, the creation of a Yugoslavia struck thoughtful people as both a noble ideal and a practical policy. Serbs, Croats, and Slovenes (Bulgars and Albanians were sometimes proposed for the mixture) were being ground down between two despotic empires ruled from Vienna and Constantinople. Hungary subjected the Croats to the humiliating (though ineffective) program of forced assimilation known as "Magyarization," while Serbs in Bosnia were oppressed first by the Turks and then by the Dual Monarchy. In addition, Slovenia (already heavily Germanized) was receiving more and more unwelcome attention from the nationalist and expansive Kingdom of Italy.

In so dangerous a world, none of these peoples, by itself, could maintain autonomy, much less sovereign independence, and "hanging together" seemed preferable to "hanging separately." Southern Slavs, it is true, were divided by religion: Slovenes and Croats were Catholic; most Serbs were Orthodox, though there were still people who regarded themselves as Serbian Catholics in Dalmatia; and much of the Serbian population of Bosnia were Muslims. But, the Yugoslavists insisted, they shared a more or less common language (though in the case of the Slovenes this was a palpable fiction) and a common culture. The cultural affinities were also exaggerated in the propaganda. Five centuries of divergent history had oriented the Serbs toward the Byzantine and post-Byzantine East and the Croats toward the cultural traditions of *Mitteleuropa*.

The first Yugoslav project came to a head during the tumults of 1848. Hungary had broken away from Austria, and Vojvodina Serbs were demanding autonomy or even independence from Hungary. The Croats, seeing a chance to get out from under the Hungarian yoke, defended the Hapsburg Empire, while calling for Croatian autonomy. In Montenegro, Njegoš did all he could to further the unification of the Serbs and willingly collaborated with Ban Jelačić in Croatia. Before and after 1848, a variety of plans for unifying the Southern Slavs were put forward by prominent 19th-century Yugoslavists such as Ilija Garašanin (Serbian prime minister), who favored unification under the Serbian crown, and Croatian nationalist leaders such as Bishop Josip Strossmayer, who promoted cultural affinities between Serbs and Croats and went so far as to advocate the transfer of Bosnia-Hercegovina to Serbian control. Strossmayer believed (quite correctly as events turned out) that Croatians were incapable of creating a state that could protect their people from a stronger Central European state (such as Hungary), but it is not at all clear that he would not have preferred to see a free Croatia under the Hapsburg crown.

Austria-Hungary's defeat in World War I eliminated the Hapsburg option, and unification was to proceed along the lines of Garašanin's famous memorandum (*Načertanije*) of 1844. Garašanin, who exchanged many letters with Njegoš, was a shrewd politician, whose primary interest lay in the creation of a Serbian state that would include all the Serbs within its borders, but he also came to believe that such a state could only defend itself if it succeeded in driving the Austrians out of the Balkans and eliminating Vienna's economic and cultural hegemony over the Southern Slavs.

During the war, a group of exiles from Croatia and Dalmatia had formed the Yugoslav Committee and established contact both with other ethnic groups in the Hapsburg dominions and with representatives of the Serbian government. Initially, however, Prime Minister Nikola Pašić was unwilling to accept the committee as the representative of Slavs in Austria-Hungary. Pašić favored expansion of the Serbian state to include traditional Serb lands, and he was skeptical of schemes to merge Serbia with a large number of the Hapsburg Empire's Slavs, whose political and cultural experiences were quite different from those of the Serbs. Who were the members of the committee, after all, that they should be entrusted with forming a state?

But in May 1917, three Slavic members of the Austro-Hungarian parliament demanded South Slavic unification under the Hapsburg crown. This alarming prospect (to say nothing of pressure from Prince Aleksandar) may have encouraged Pašić to come to terms with the Yugoslav Committee, which he invited to a meeting in Corfu. For six weeks, they held discussions, which resulted in the Declaration of Corfu calling for a Yugoslav state under the Serbian crown. Although the participants had debated the question of a centralized *versus* a federal state, the declaration left the question to be solved by the South Slav Constituent Assembly. In fact, it was never solved.[3]

Foreign critics of Yugoslavia have suggested that it was folly to expect such quarrelsome and violent peoples to live within a single state, but this is a Western condescension that borders on xenophobia. North Americans and Western Europeans have had problems of their own: the American Civil War (fought largely between British Protestants); the Quebec separatist movement in Canada; the Ulster question, which flames into violence more frequently than the Balkans; to say nothing of the persistent friction between Flemings and Walloons in Belgium or the social and political conflict in Italy between *Polentoni* ("Big Polentas") north of the Po and *Terroni* ("Big Dirts") in the South. Even in the United States, the wounds created by the War Between the States are not entirely healed.[4]

No, what the Yugoslavists did not take into consideration was human nature. Human beings are just as prone to define themselves by what they hate as by what they love, and in the absence of an immediate common threat, people who differ only slightly will fight over that slight difference. If an Irishman has no foreigner to fight, it is said, he will fight another Irishman, but the Irish have often fought each other even as they were being attacked by foreigners. Yugoslav idealists have much in common with those who advocate multiethnic/multicultural states, in defiance of history and of the common sense embedded in Karl Schmitt's repeated observation that political life is organized along the coordinates of the friend/enemy distinction. In a part of the world so diverse in ethnicity and religion, there is no end of enemies to organize against.

Organizing the Multiethnic State

The first Yugoslavia was a unitary, rather than a federal, state constructed on a French model. The country was divided, not into the historic regions and ethnicities from which it was formed, but into 30 administrative districts whose purpose was to prevent the emergence of ethnic separatism.

Between 1918 and the outbreak of World War II, the rulers of Yugoslavia were primarily occupied with the problem of Croatia. While many Croats had supported the Yugoslav idea, their conception usually took the form of a federal state in which an autonomous Croatia could recover a sense of cultural and national identity. Serb leaders, including Prince-Regent (later King) Aleksandar and Prime Minister Nikola Pašić, were convinced that only a unitary state on the centralized French model could keep the lid on the boiling pot of ethnic tensions.

The leaders of the Croatian Peasant Party went almost immediately into an opposition that bordered on treason. Stjepan Radić was telling the Serbs from the beginning that Croats had little interest in the glorious traditions of Kosovo and Karadjordje, and he played a dangerous political game throughout the 1920's, blowing hot and cold on cooperation with the Belgrade government. In 1928 Radić, along with several other Croatian members of parliament, was shot by a Montenegrin deputy, Puniša Račić, and when Vladko Maček, his successor, continued to play the same game, upping the ante at every turn, the country was on the brink of anarchy.

Macek and Svetozar Pribićević (a Serb from Croatia who had been vice president of the National Committee in Zagreb) proposed a division of the country into seven districts, which would have had the effect of cutting off Montenegro and Vojvodina from Serbia. This reorganization was not proposed out of respect for Montenegro's own state traditions, but as a scheme to divide the Serbs and strengthen the Croats (thus binding them more closely to the Yugoslav state). King Aleksandar appears to

have thought of offering the Croats their independence in order to concentrate on building up a Serbian kingdom. In the end, however, the king
proclaimed a dictatorship (in 1929) and tried his best to restore order and
encourage unity, but to no avail. Responding to constant pressure from
Croats, Slovenes, and Montenegrins, the king broke the kingdom into abstract regions (*banovine*) formed along major river valleys.

Croatian Ustaša terrorists had him assassinated in 1934, and for the
rest of the decade the Serbian government would prove itself unable to
deal with Croatian separatists, who were being supported by Fascist
Italy.[5] The Sporazum (agreement) signed in 1939, which created an autonomous greater Croatia that included Slavonia, Dalmatia, and parts of
Bosnia-Hercegonia, though giving the 77 percent Croat majority the right
to rule Serbs and Muslims, only whetted the nationalist appetites.

Troubles in Montenegro

Although the Serbian government had taken Montenegro's support
for unification as a given, not all Montenegrins were happy with the new
arrangement. They had not even been represented on Corfu, when the
Yugoslav Committee drew up plans for the new state. Although most
Montenegrins favored unification, some would have preferred to see a
more federal arrangement under which Montenegro and its royal dynasty were given the same status as Bavaria within Germany. There were
many motives for discontent. "Some," wrote Milovan Djilas, "were supporters of King Nikola," who longed for independence.

> There were, however, others who were not satisfied with the way
> the unification was being effected—through occupation. Then
> there were many dissatisfied peasants, men whom the war had
> uprooted from their previous lives and occupations, who looked
> to the others, not knowing what else to do. There were other men
> who were dissatisfied but did not themselves know quite why;
> they were caught up by the rebellious times.

The confusion of the time is illustrated by Djilas's own father, one of
King Nikola's officers but no enthusiast for the dynast. He was afraid
that an uneducated Montenegrin could not succeed in the Yugoslav army.
He also felt that Montenegrin pride was being humiliated:

Some Serbians called the Montenegrins traitors [because of the collapse in 1916] and threw up into their faces that they, the Serbians, had liberated them. The Serbians sang mocking songs, one about how the wives of each had greeted the Austrians—the Serbian women with bombs, the Montenegrin women with breasts.[6]

In the Brda, where resentments were still smoldering against Nikola, there were celebrations of the union, but in Katuni, the home region of the Monenegrin capital, unification was widely viewed as a hostile takeover by Serbia. A number of Prince Nikola's former officers and retainers wanted to restore national sovereignty and, more to the point, the Montenegrin sovereign. Instigated and financially assisted by the Italian government, a conspiracy of Nikola's officers and officials staged an insurrection on Christmas Eve of 1919. The chief ringleader was "Prime Minister in Exile" Jovan Plamenac, a diehard supporter of Nikola and the former minister of the interior who had prosecuted the "bombers."

In Cetinje, there was some hard fighting in which 16 Whites and their Serbian allies were killed and 63 wounded. Informed of the Christmas uprising, an embittered King Nikola remarked that Montenegro would not be taken like a bride without a dowry. Although the rebellion was quickly put down, largely for lack of support among the people, there were the usual reprisals. Throughout the 1920's, chauvinists and irredentists, who had followed the ancestral custom and taken to the hills, cultivated the traditional profession of tax resistance and banditry. There was even a Communist presence among the zelanaši, Dr. Vukašin Marković, who had come back from Russia (where he had joined the Bolsheviks) to his native Piperi.[7]

Montenegrins overwhelmingly supported the union, but many were not content to see their country merged totally into Serbia. They quite naturally wanted a Montenegrin province with its own identity but within a federal union. Some who had stayed out of trouble reentered politics in 1925 on a federalist platform. The party's theoretician, Sekula Drljević, publicly professed allegiance to Yugoslav unity but only to a union of recognized states that preserved their pre-1917 frontiers. These "federalists" were numerous enough to give concern to King Aleksandar, who (as part of the reorganization undertaken in 1929) established the Zetska Banovina with its own borders, local government (under a *ban*), and identity, but this was not enough for Drljević, who championed Montenegrin identity under a decidedly fascist—or rather Ustaša—flag, arguing that racially the Montenegrins were Illyrian rather than Slavic.[8]

The Making of Nations: Red Croatia

It was during the interwar period that the ideology of Montenegrin political and cultural separatism was born. The theory was not a native production, but a cuckoo introduced into the Montenegrin nest from Vienna by way of Zagreb. Montenegrin racetheory (which is what it is) was simply an extension of Grof Benjamin von Kallay's strategy of fragmenting the Serbs and feeding the fragments to the Hapsburg Empire or a designated successor to its ambitions. In the case of Montenegro, the strategy was a total failure until after World War II, when it was co-opted into the official ideology of Tito's regime and imposed with the full force and power of the communist state.

No ethnic group and certainly no small nation has ever been exempt from jealousy and sensitivity, and it is usually an easy matter to persuade members of a minority that all their problems stem from prejudice and persecution. Montenegrins were also potentially vulnerable to such strategic deception, because, like most Serbs, they took pride in their regional distinctiveness, though no more so, perhaps, than Serbs from Krajina, whom Austria converted into Gränzer. Other ethnic inventions were the "Bosniaks" (Muslim Serbs of Bosnia-Hercegovina), the Macedonians, and, more recently the "Kosovars" (Albanian Muslims whose immigration into Kosovo was encouraged first by the Turks and then by Tito).[9]

Austro-Hungarian creativity in the art of ethnogenesis had not gone so far as to invent a Montenegrin nation. To divide Montenegro and Serbia, Vienna had preferred to incite dynastic and political differences between Belgrade and Cetinje. At the end of World War I, however, the ethnogenesis project was maintained by Croat writers, who—when they were not forging alternative histories of the "Iranian Croats"—were busily constructing race myths to divide the Serbs or reduce them to the level of *Untermenschen*.

Ivo Pilar, the Croatian nationalist who wrote under the *nom-de-plume* "Südland," was the first to grasp the potential significance of Montenegro's particularism. In his 1918 anti-Serb pamphlet, *"Die Südslawische Frage und der Weltkrieg"* ("The South Slavic Question and the World War," reprinted in Croatian in 1943 and 1993!), Pilar was not bold enough to invent a separate "Montenegrin nation," but he did try to convert Montenegrins into crypto-Westerners, separated from the Serbs by Theodosius' division of the empire in A.D. 395 along the line going from Belgrade to Scutari. Pilar was partly relying on the Bavarian historian and German nationalist Jakob Philipp Fallmerayer, who claimed that Montenegrins were of mainly Albanian and other pre-Slavic stock.

For obvious political reasons, Pilar set out to prove that the Montenegrins were of pre-Slavic and "Red Croat" descent. Red Croatia, whose shadowy existence is known only from the *Duklja Chronicle*, was either a fantasy of the Latin Catholic "Pop" or, just as likely, a later addition to the text. Whatever he chose to believe about Red Croatia, Pilar was forced to concede that, by the 11th century, the Serb element in Montenegro was, regrettably, already beginning to prevail, and he did not even try to pretend that 20th-century Montenegrins were anything but Serbs.[10]

That fiction was first attempted in the 1930's, both by the Communist Party of Yugoslavia and by a Montenegrin ally of the Croatian Ustaša movement, Savić Marković (nicknamed "Štedimlija"), who simply borrowed Pilar's arguments and "research" in order to prove that Montenegrins were not Serbs at all. While Pilar had attempted to solve all questions of South Slavic identity in a way favorable to Croatian aspirations, Štedimlija, in copying Pilar, confined himself to the Montenegrin question. Štedimlija's 1937 brochure, "The Basis of Montenegrin Nationalism" (*"Osnovi crnogorskog nacionalizma"*) provided both Communists and Ustaše with their fundamental theory.

Štedimlija borrows Pilar's "Red Croatia" race myth and goes much further in aligning Montenegro with the West, explaining away the apparent contradiction—that most Montenegrins were proud Serbs—as a mere political tactic adopted to protect Montenegrin independence. However, despite the layers of Serbian false consciousness, he says, geography has imposed an essentially Western character. "Closed from the north and east by tall mountains . . . Montenegro has always been open only to the sea, and, to some extent, to the West via Hercegovina." At best, such a description could be applied to the Zeta Valley and the Littoral, but most of today's Montenegro is oriented toward the Lim Valley, and from 1499 until 1878 it had no access to the sea. Although Old Montenegro had far stronger links with Brda and with Serbia than it ever had with the Littoral, Štedimlija insisted that "the old population of Montenegro was able to bring the seeds of Western culture to its midst and to subject itself to that culture's influence."

Like most ideologues, Štedimlija had an answer for every obstacle that history and reality might put in his way. In calling themselves Serbs, he said, Montenegrins were partly falling under the influence of immigrants from Rascia, but they were also willing to identify with the legacy of Nemanja, who was, after all, a man from Zeta. They also accepted the Kosovo myth promoted by new waves of Serbian immigrants, he explained, because it was not enslaved Serbs but the victorious Turks who posed a threat to Montenegro.

The unyielding obstacle to all the racetheories that underlie the claims of Montenegrin separatists is the Serbian patriotism of Bishop Danilo, St. Petar, Bishop Njegoš, Prince Danilo, and King Nikola. In the case of Njegoš, Štedimlija argues that his attempt to represent himself as a loyal Serb was simply a ploy, but his mental outlook as a "pure Westerner" is apparent from his poetry. Anyone who has read Njegoš understands what a palpable lie this is.

Unfortunately, this argument has far more resonance today than in the 1930's, when Montenegrins knew their own traditions. The truth is that Montenegrin "nationalists," if they are to succeed in throwing off the burden of being Serbian, must repudiate the entire history and culture of Montenegro. For those who wish to demonize the Serbs, Njegoš is the enemy, and so long as Montenegrins maintain a connection with the past, they will be viewed as the enemy.[11]

Already in the 1930's, Štedimlija was predicting a brilliant future for Montenegro, whenever it would "shake off from its face the layers of dead historical dust deposited by the centuries of unpleasantness." The elimination of Serbian identity (all that dead dust) would be the ticket to the New European Order soon to be forged by two great Western nations, and standing ready to assist the Axis powers in reconstructing Montenegro was their junior partner, Croatia, which is "more than a nation: it is the synonym for all that is good and beautiful in the creation of the European West."

The logical conclusion of this reasoning came after the proclamation of the Independent State of Croatia, when Štedimlija and his political mentor Sekula Drljević established a "Montenegrin National Committee" sponsored and paid for by Ante Pavelić, the Ustaša leader. At the end of the war, Štedimlija was captured by the Soviets, delivered to Tito, tried, given a token sentence (at a time when " Četnik" heads were rolling by the thousands), and almost immediately released. He was subsequently employed at the Lexographic Institute in Zagreb, under the guidance of Miroslav Krleža, a Croat writer with unusually close ties to Tito. He died of old age, enjoying a well-earned pension from Tito. He never changed his views on the character of Montenegro, but after 1945 those views were easily repackaged to be part of Tito's anti-Serb Yugoslavism.

Red Montenegro

On the communist side, the earliest known mention of the "Montenegrin Question" is found in a 1926 issue of *Borba*, the Communist Party of Yugoslavia (CPY) organ published in Zagreb. Borba's editor, Ante Ciliga, became the secretary of the Communist Party of Croatia, who switched sides 1941 to become secretary to Pavelić's minister of education. The first reference to "Montenegri-nation" came at the fourth congress of the CPY in Dresden (1928), which also advocated the creation of an independent and united Albania (including Kosovo, of course) and the demolition of the "greater-Serbian Versailles creation, Yugoslavia." By 1934 the CPY was demanding the expulsion of "Serbian occupiers" from Croatia, Slovenia, Dalmatia, Vojvodina, Bosnia, Kosovo—and Montenegro.[12]

The party was later forced to retreat from its extreme "Serbo-phobia" when it was instructed to pursue the "Popular Front" policy during the war. The Anti-Fascist Council for Yugoslavia (AVNOJ) took up the ethnic question at its second session in November 1943. Moša Pijade argued for a series of autonomous Serbian territories, but this conceded too much to ethnicity and religion. Instead, Yugoslavia ultimately (1945) established separate republics of Croatia, Slovenia, Serbia, Macedonia, Bosnia, and Montenegro.

War, Occupation, Civil War

Štedimlija's race fantasies made little headway in Montenegro, where the old generation of opponents to unification was dying out. Some Montenegrins naturally wanted greater recognition for their historic identity, but whether federalism was the answer to Yugoslavia's ethnic questions will never be known, since Serbs and Croats were soon swept into the general European maelstrom.

Yugoslav policy toward Germany in the 1930's was at best ambivalent and, after the March coup, confused and vacillating. The country's military establishment was barely large enough to cope with the Italians, much less with Hitler's *Wehrmacht*, but Serbs, conscious of their brave tra-ditions, were in favor of standing up to German bullying. Through his ambassador in Berlin, Ivo Andrić, Prime Minister Cvetković warned the Germans that if Yugoslavia were forced to sign the Tripartite Pact, there would be an uprising, but Hitler was adamant. From the other side, Cvetković was receiving pressure from the Allies to commit national suicide by standing up to Nazi Germany.[13]

In January 1941, Colonel William "Wild Bill" Donovan, the chief of the OSS and godfather to the CIA, had arrived in Belgrade to bring President Roosevelt's encouragement. After meeting with Donovan, Cvetković observed:

> Col. Donovan proved to be one in a line of experts who display total ignorance of the particular problems of the country they are visiting . . . Very superficially informed of Yugoslavia, which he was visiting for the first time—not knowing its language, its history, traditions, mentality, its political, economic and military situation—such a man could not form a proper idea of the problems of Yugoslavia in a few days . . . He did not know a thing about the Balkans.[14]

Donovan was to be followed by future American experts, especially in the 1990's, when Warren Zimmerman, Richard Holbrooke, and Madeleine Albright plotted the dismemberment of a country and the destruction of a people.

When Prince-Regent Pavle's strategy of cautious accommodation was reversed by a coup at the end of March 1941, the Axis powers declared war on Yugoslavia. The March 27 coup was led by Generals Dušan Simović and Bora Mirković. Simović was an officer with good connections. He had been made the royal aide-de-camp after World War I. In 1918, as Lt. Col. Simović, he was in Podgorica, at the head of Serb forces, to help ensure the desired outcome at the National Assembly. But although the new government was careful not to offend Germany and succeeded in extracting a promise from Maček to join the cabinet, Hitler saw his chance to punish the Serbs for "starting World War I." The Germans attacked with great force in early April, but Hitler reserved his most devastating assault for Belgrade itself. Croatia, which had declared independence and was now an "independent" ally of Italy and Germany, was spared, and the rest of Yugoslavia was divided up among the Axis powers.[15]

The Royal Yugoslav Army did have one success, and that was on the Scutari (Skadar) front, where the Zeta Division, a largely Montenegrin unit commanded by popular World War I veteran Gen. Milenko Varjačić, attacked the Italians and Albanians as soon as war was declared. They reached the outskirts of Scutari, and when the armistice of April 17 was announced, they left their positions with tears in their eyes, denouncing "the betrayal of the Croats," which they believed had made the German advance possible.

The hastily cobbled together system of occupation was plagued by disagreements between Italy and Germany. While the Italians were willing to make deals on the ground with the lesser of two evils (*i.e.*, non-Communist guerillas), Hitler wanted to impose a Carthaginian peace on all the Serbs, but the Germans were unable to allocate the resources to maintain so harsh an order. German brutality (to say nothing of the abominations committed openly in Croatian territory) created resistance that German manpower could not entirely suppress. The turmoil in the Balkans was becoming an annoyance for Hitler at a time when he was preparing to invade the Soviet Union, and the annoyance was about to turn into aggravation.

Hitler's decision to invade the U.S.S.R. (June 22, 1941) brought the Communist Party of Yugoslavia into the war. Communist recruiters were able to invoke (however cynically) the image of "Mother Russia" as the friend of the Serbs. It must have been difficult for a Communist to follow the twists and turns of Comintern instructions in those days. In the spring of 1941, Communists seemed ready to accept the new order, and they considered the possibility of legalizing a "Communist Party of the Independent State of Croatia." Some Communists had joined the demonstrations against Prince Paul that brought down the government, but they joined late and were later reproved by Tito. (After the war, it is said, clocks had to excised from photographs of the demonstrations, because they indicated how late the Communists were in showing up.)

Communist support for the Axis division of Yugoslavia had to be abandoned when Germany invaded the U.S.S.R. At that point, the Comintern declared in favor of reestablishing the independence and territorial integrity of Yugoslavia. Until the mid-1930's, the YCP had opposed the very existence of the Yugoslav state, to the point of expressing support for the Ustaša movement, whose members they tried to lure into the party fold.

To Italy's share fell Montenegro and Dalmatia (in addition to Albania, which the Italians had taken in 1939). Serbs under Italian rule were comparatively welloff, and many survivors of the war have fondly recalled the kindness of Italian military authorities. Many Royal Yugoslav Army soldiers and officers were not taken prisoner but allowed to go home. Italians also protected Serbs and Jews from the genocide directed at them from the Croatian government of Ante Pavelić.

If the Italians expected to win over the Montenegrins with kindness—and the restoration of their independent monarchy—they were to be sadly disappointed. There was little support for the *zelenaši* (Greens) by 1941, and that little was largely the nostalgia of men too old to fight. Even the leader of the Federalists, Savo Vuletić, refused to take part in the independence movement, insisting that he had always favored a federal union of Serbia and Montenegro.[16]

In April, nonetheless, a group of exiles and supporters of Nikola met in Tirana and convened the Committee for the Creation of an Independent Montenegro, and in early May, Italian authorities began taking over the reins of government. Mussolini failed to find a Petrović heir foolish enough to volunteer to serve as puppet ruler. After casting about, the Italians settled upon Prince Mihailo, Nikola's grandson, who was actually a firm believer in the union of Montenegro and Serbia. Mihailo refused the offer (according to Italian Foreign Minister Count Ciano on June 7, 1941) because "he is convinced that in the end Germany and Italy will be beaten, and for this reason he considers that any present solution is transitory and ephemeral."

The Italian government, nonetheless, was encouraged by a handful of Greens and proceeded with plans to proclaim (on July 12) an independent kingdom as an Italian protectorate. In his brief term of office, the civil governor, Conte Serafino Mazzolini (1890-1945), established a "central commission" composed of old separatists like Petar Plamenac and Mihailo Ivanović, who persuaded him to appoint Sekula Drljević as Montenegro's "prime minister." Drljević, who arrived hurriedly from Zagreb, only inspired loathing among the already disaffected Montenegrins. Drljević was soon at odds with royalists who wanted to set up a Council of Regents that would have royal prerogatives. In contrast, Drljević and Ivanović did not care what form the government took, so long as Montenegro was "independent," even if it meant total subservience to Italy.

The Italians hoped to rely on the popularity of the Montenegrin queen of Italy in her native land, but their plans for a peaceful occupation were not helped by the decision to transfer to "Greater Albania" some areas liberated by Montenegro in the First Balkan War (western Metohija, including Peć and Dečani), as well as a strip of territory that had belonged to Montenegro ever since 1878 (Ulcinj and the Malesija region along the Albanian border near Podgorica). Italy's direct annexation of the Boka all the way to Budva was particularly painful.

As soon as the agitation for independence started, a group of loyal officers started making informal contact with their classmates all over Montenegro, and with other prominent local people, preparing for insurrection. The leaders of this network were General Djukanović, Capt. Pavle Djurišić, Col. Bajo Stanišić, and Capt. Djordjije Lašić. Perhaps no one on either side anticipated the violence of the uprising that took place on July 13 (St. Peter's Day or Petrovdan), the day after Montenegro's declaration of independence. Ciano (July 14) was stunned:

> Disorders in Montenegro. Shooting by armed bands, an assault on the royal villa in Budva. It appears that his has no connection with the constituent assembly, but the coincidence of events is at least strange.

Ciano was soon disabused. Two thousand Italian soldiers were killed, and most of the country taken back. The irony of Montenegro, supposedly loyal to the queen of Italy, in rebellion was not lost on Ciano (July 17): "The Montenegrin insurrection . . . is assuming greater proportions. If it did not have a deep and bitter significance, it would be grotesque that war exists between Italy and Montenegro."

The uprising seems to have unhinged Mazzolini, who fled to Italy "for consultations." (At the end of the war, he was murdered by the Communists.) Within two days, Kolašin, Andrijevica, Virpazar, Berane, Bijelo Polje, Šavnik, and other places were liberated, and local Italian garrisons either surrendered or retreated to the coast. By July 24, Mussolini seems to have realized that the separatist scenario was a non-starter. He fired Drljević, who, after being interned by the Italians, was allowed to escape to Zagreb, never to step on Montenegrin soil again. The High Commission was dissolved, and the members sought refuge in Italian barracks or went into hiding. All civil and military authority was entrusted to Gen. Alessandro Pirzio-Biroli, who had earned his spurs in the "pacification" of Abyssynia. Montenegro was occupied by the XIV Army Corps of the 9th Italian Army, which was equivalent to about three divisions for a small country with under 400,000 people. This was the highest ratio of occupying troops to local population in the war.

The Italians were shocked by the violence. Their officers, who had expected to be welcomed as liberators, were horrified by the sporadic atrocities committed, usually by Communist detachments, on Italian prisoners. News of the executions stiffened the resolve of Italian soldiers, who were initially inclined to throw down their arms and surrender as soon as a few shots were fired. Although the Italian army's counterattack took thousands of lives, the casualties largely fell into the modern American category of "collateral damage" as a result of artillery shelling and aerial strafing. The Italians did not adopt the *Wehrmacht's* tactic in Serbia, where they shot a hundred innocent hostages for every German soldier killed.

The Communists, led by Milovan Djilas and Arso Jovanović (a trained officer from the Royal Yugoslav Army) arrived to attempt to take over a rebellion they had neither planned nor could control. Students were shipped in from Belgrade and sent home to take over the insurrection. They played upon the old ties with Russia, and it was genuinely believed that the Russians would push back the Germans within weeks. Such delusions were actively promoted by the party, which also claimed that Russian parachutists were already present in some districts. The magic worked, and those fiery-eyed youngsters with bizarre ideas were suddenly taken seriously by their neighbors, solely on the strength of the connections they claimed to have with Moscow.

Josip Broz "Tito" had wanted a series of small actions, inviting Italian reprisals that would create sympathy for the Communists. What happened was the worst-case scenario for Tito: a genuinely popular uprising mounted by people who were neither loyal to the party nor imbued with Marxist ideology. Djilas could not make him understand that Montenegrins were not like Slovenes or even Serbs from Serbia, and Tito dismissed him from his position as leader in the Montenegrin Party.

Montenegro did produce many communists who fought with Tito's *Partizani*, though for a variety of motives. Some were still loyal to Russia, now a Communist state; others had been indoctrinated as students — some of them of the perpetual student type that has become so familiar; others were simply attracted to the political party that promised them guns and the chance to emulate the exploits of their fathers and grandfathers.

The Montenegrins were a puzzle to the Communists, and *vice versa.* What must the peasants have made of Uncle Janko, the name adopted by communist theoretician and *avant-garde* painter Moša Pijade? More at home in a Belgrade café than in the country, Pijade was a Jewish intellectual who took Marxist ideology seriously, and while war was breaking out all over, Uncle Janko was setting up a collective farm on Mt. Durmitor and keeping detailed Soviet-style inventory of livestock and personnel. The Montenegrin Djilas, more poet than ideologue, was equally delusional. Depressed at his failures in Montenegro, his spirits were restored by a picnic on Crno Jezero (near Žabljak on Durmitor):

> We took cover in a stand of fir trees. I took out a saddlebag of ham I had brought as a treat for Tito, and Tito, Arso Jovanović, and I had a feast, while a plane showered machine-gun fire all around us. The delicious food, the bright sky, and Tito's self-confidence restored my good humor."[17]

By July 22, Ciano realized things were getting worse as the Montenegrin rebels were being reinforced by Serbs (and even Croats, according to Ciano). The Italians sent reinforcements, who came up the well-traveled path of Turkish expeditions, from Scutari to Podgorica, then into the mountains. The three columns that advanced on Cetinje, Nikšić, and Kolašin demolished all the houses that lay along the roads. In early August, the Italians stirred up the Montenegrins' ancient enemies, Albanians and Turkish Muslims of Sanjak, who were happy to settle old scores by going on a rampage of burning and looting. By late August the Italians had interned some 26,000 Montenegrins, mostly men. In fact, just over ten percent of the entire male population was made prisoners. About 10,000 were taken to Italy to perform forced labor.

The Partisans in retreat now began "executing" (that is, murdering) their rivals (both separatist Greens and the noncommunist Chetniks) to ensure that postwar Montenegro would have no bourgeois leadership to resist a communist takeover. In Croatia, the CPY leaders expressed their satisfaction that the Ustašas had "done the job" for the communists by liquidating the local Serbian "establishment." In Montenegro, they had to do the job themselves. They proceeded with it as soon as the Italians withdrew to their fortifications along the coast.

Throughout their history, Montenegrins have endured (and inflicted upon each other) almost unbelievable horrors, but the Communists, in annihilating entire families of "class enemies," broke new ground. Early in the campaign, the Communists attacked the Jovović family in the Piperi. They killed Djuro Jovović, the head of the family, his three sons, Nikola, Šćepan, and Toko, as well as Toko's and Nikola's wives. Two of Djuro's nephews, Radovan and Milovan Jovović, who happened to be in the house, were killed for daring to protest the slaughter they had witnessed.[18] Since the liquidation of "class enemies" was a proof of party loyalty, Partisan commanders and local party cadres entered into competition to produce the highest number of murders.

In the third week of December 1941, after a huge snowfall made it impossible to supply isolated garrisons, the Italians evacuated Kolašin, Mojkovac, and Šavnik. When Serb "nationalists" established their authority in Kolašin, there was a brief spell of peace, until Partisans attacked the city on Orthodox Christmas Eve (January 6, 1942) with 1,000 men. Heavily outgunned and outnumbered, the nationalists had to withdraw.

The Communists were then in a position to carry out the plan they had prepared. They first patrolled the streets announcing that nobody was to leave his home; any movement in the streets, would be immediately punished by death. The chairman of the Communist court-martial, Savo Brković, had already selected a plot of land in the nearby hamlet of Kolašinski Lug. His men took a stray dog, nailed it to a Badnjak (the yule log with straw and oak leaves) in the middle of the field, and named it the Graveyard of Dogs (Pasje groblje). Partisan patrols led by the perpetual students Boško Rašović and Vukman Kruščić then proceeded from one marked home to another, arresting their designated victims, who were mostly prominent and respectable people, doctors and officers, teachers, judges, civil servants, and priests. They were condemned as kulaks, spies, enemies of the revolution, even Trockists, whatever that might have meant in Kolašin.[19]

That same evening, in the light of burning torches, they executed over 200 people out of a population of only 3,000, killing them with hammer blows, in front of the bloodied Badnjak on which the dog still squealed in agony. Their bodies were dumped into shallow graves, where they were later preyed upon by animals. While one group of communists was carrying out the slaughter, another herded the survivors into the high school auditorium where they were forced to take part in a "People's Feast" (a sort of anti-Christmass), singing and dancing to drown out the screams and groans that echoed through the night from the drowned field beside the Tara River. Relatives were forbidden to approach the field of horrors, though 350 bodies were eventually recovered by the Chetniks seven weeks later and buried with Christian rites.

The following morning, on Christmas Day, Communists began arresting people who were not on the initial liquidation list, mainly members of families of nationalist guerrillas who had left the city. They were beating them on the way to jail and killing some in full sight of the horrified citizens. Some of them were then taken to the nearby village of Rečine, where a Chetnik detachment commanded by the local district judge, Ljubo Minić, was entrenched in a few sturdy houses. They pushed trembling women and children ahead and threatened to kill them one by one unless the Chetniks surrendered. Those who did surrender were killed. The others retreated into the Vasojević villages, where they were warmly greeted and were able to recruit volunteers.[20]

Communist plans for imposing a complete reign of terror on the liberated areas were frustrated by the return from Ravna Gora of Capt. Pavle Djurišić in the first week of January 1942. Djurišić, one of the leaders of the July uprising, went to Draža Mihailović's headquarters seeking instructions on how to confront the escalating communist violence. Upon his return, he skillfully organized Chetnik formations and transformed the "nationalists," loosely defined as opponents of both Italian occupation and the communists, into detachments of the Yugoslav Army in the Homeland.

On February 21, 1942, Djurišić's new army moved against the communist stronghold in Kolašin, which they took after a day of fierce fighting. Up to this point, disputes between nationalists and communists were conducted with varying degrees of hostility, but when the Chetniks viewed firsthand the Graveyard of Dogs, they grew determined to pursue the retreating communists, who were given no quarter. After the Dogs' Graveyard, neither side took prisoners.

Other notorious locations of communist crimes were the Kotor Hole (Kotor Jama), a hole in the rocky hills near Nikšić, where about 500 people were thrown from the region of Old Hercegovina, and the Kecina Hole near the Partisan headquarters for Montenegro. About 300 people were shot at its edge, or even thrown alive into the 350-foot-deep pit.

Emboldened by the communist defeat, people all over Montenegro and eastern Hercegovina started an all-out hunt for "Moša's bastards" (*Mošina kopilad*). By the spring of 1942, the Partizani were comprehensively routed, but their route to Sanjak and Serbia was blocked at Kolašin, and their remnants escaped to Bosnia.

The conditions were so favorable to the Chetnik insurgents that Draža Mihailović established his headquarters in northern Montenegro in early 1942 when German pressure forced his retreat from Serbia. Following the failed communist attempt to revive operations by attacking Pljevlja (December 1941), which was the last major engagement of the uprising, they were expelled from Montenegro, and relative peace reigned in most parts until the spring of 1943.

The Partisans' policy of exterminating all real, potential, or imagined "class enemies" had bred animosity in many people who were initially sympathetic to them as friends of the Russians. Their frenzied attempt to kill as many "reactionaries" (teachers, priests, lawyers, doctors, officers, local administrators, "kulaks," etc.) as they could was rooted in their genuine conviction that war would be over in months and that it was necessary to prepare the ground for their own postwar rule. Already in October, the CPY named Mihailović as "the main danger to the successful development of the people's liberation struggle."[21]

After the failed attack on Pljevlja, the Partisan command in Montenegro instructed all their units to refrain from attacking Italians and to concentrate all their forces on fighting Chetniks, and this policy was subsequently approved by Tito himself.[22] By the spring of 1942, the Communists had lost the first round of the civil war that they had instigated, with the Italians remaining on the sidelines, or—in some cases— helping local Chetnik units with arms and supplies.

When defeated remnants of communist units withdrew to Bosnia, an informal truce was established that prevailed for well over a year. Heavily armed Italian convoys would wearily make their way from the coast to fortified garrisons, not veering left or right from the main roads. The Chetniks in the surrounding hills would let them pass, realizing that the *status quo* was preferable to the ever-present threat of Germans and Albanians coming to complete the job if the Italians found themselves in trouble yet again. The main objective of the uprising had been achieved, however: No further attempt was made by the Italians to revive the idea of Montenegrin independence.

When the Italians had counterattacked late in the summer of 1941, they discovered that the most determined opposition came from the communists. The Italian military governor, Gen. A. Pirzio Biroli, was well aware of this cleavage between communist and noncommunist Montenegrins, and by the autumn of 1941 he was already putting out secret feelers to local Chetnik leaders, offering to leave them and their men undisturbed in the countryside, provided they would in turn not attack the Italian garrisons and communications.

The Chetnik leaders accepted, and this was the beginning of a pragmatic understanding between Italians and Chetniks. This was not genuine "collaboration," since the two sides had entirely different objectives. From the Chetnik side, cooperation was a local necessity, not a decision made at the top.[23] Mihailović was still in Serbia and had limited control over events in Montenegro, where local Chetnik leaders were acting independently.

Three groups of Chetniks were fighting independently in Montenegro under the command of individual Yugoslav army officers who were not (except for Pavle Djurišić) coordinating their activities with each other or with headquarters. Though there were attempts at mounting a joint resistance, the Partisans and Chetniks were fighting each other before the end of 1941. The civil war between Chetniks and Partisans was nowhere more brutal than in Montenegro, where ideological distinctions took on the coloring of a vendetta between rival clans.

After the Communists were driven out, the interior of Montenegro became a Chetnik redoubt, except for a few cities and the coastline, which the Italians controlled. For his part, Mihailović avoided any direct contact with the Italians, although the British were encouraging him to take advantage of their possible withdrawal or surrender, but Mihailović operated mainly outside the Italian zone in 1941-42.

The Italians, disenchanted with Berlin's insistence on a strictly military solution to the war in the Balkans, offered little support to the Germans during their operations in eastern Bosnia in early 1942. Quite apart from their rivalries and jealousies, Germans and Italians clashed over basic strategy. While the Italians were willing to pursue peaceful coexistence with the Chetniks, the Germans viewed the Chetniks as a major problem in the event of an Allied operation in the Balkans. Hitler was concerned enough to send a letter to Mussolini (delivered by Ribbentrop in February 1943). Hitler underscored the potential danger that the Chetniks might present and requested the Duce to halt all shipments of supplies immediately:

> If we do not succeed in disarming the Communists and Chetniks to the same degree . . . then at the moment of invasion, disorder will break out, all links with Peloponnese will be cut off or interrupted, the few German divisions will be busy fighting the

Communists and Chetniks, and Italian troops will no longer be able to halt the invasion.

The growing strength of the resistance forces was felt even more by Germany's Croatian and Italian allies, who had abandoned extensive areas of the countryside to the irregulars and restricted themselves to securing the larger centers of population and the main roads and rail lines. The occupation system was in tatters, and the treatment of the Chetniks became a matter of sharp contention between German and Italian commanders during the course of Operation Weiss (the "Battle of Neretva," in Titoist historiography). In fact, the Italians had been requested to disarm their Chetnik auxiliaries as part of the third stage of that operation, but they refused to do so. According to the official U.S. Army history of the war in the Balkans,

> Large concentrations of Chetniks, including those supported by the Italians, formed a constant threat to German forces in the event of an Allied landing, and the Commander-in-Chief, Southeast, directed that Operation SCHWARZ, under the Commander of Troops in Croatia, be undertaken in May and June to destroy the Chetniks in Hercegovina and Montenegro . . . With both Yugoslav and Greek guerrillas withdrawn from large-scale operations for the moment, the Germans hastened to take steps to secure the Balkans against a threatening Italian collapse or surrender.

Hitler was right not to trust the Chetniks. Their partnership with the Italians was one of necessity, not choice, and it would have ended with the landing of the first British company in Montenegro or Dalmatia.[24] Some Chetnik commanders even admitted as much to the Italians, who must have already suspected something similar. Ciano (January 6, 1943) agreed with the Germans, but he was also aware that "in order to carry out the German plan of extermination, we need a great many more troops than both we and Germany can afford."

The Italian commanders persisted in supporting the Chetniks (even to the point of defying Mussolini's orders). Their motives may have undergone an evolution between 1941, when they were looking for allies against the Partisans and expressed sympathy for Serbs who were being persecuted by Communists and Ustaše alike, and 1943, when their primary desire may have been to exploit the Chetniks' links with the British.

The overthrow of Mussolini made it very uncomfortable for Italians in the Balkans, especially once the Germans began arresting Italian officers who refused to pledge their loyalty to Hitler.[25] Surrender to the British must have seemed like a dream, compared with the frightening alternative.[25]

General Pirzio-Biroli actually sent a message to Mihailović as early as late 1942, saying he wanted a separate peace with the British. Mihailović passed this on to London, but Anthony Eden decided against "pursuing any of these contacts." By July 1943, the Germans did not believe Badoglio's assurances that Italy would fight on. In view of the Allied landings in Sicily, the Communists were determined to make certain that no Chetnik forces would be along the Adriatic to pave the way for the Allies.

The German prospect of victory had begun to fade by the beginning of 1943. Stalingrad would cost the Germans 22 divisions by February, and Axis forces in North Africa would be forced to surrender to the Allies in May. The growing losses on all fronts could no longer be replaced in full, and Fortress Europe was threatened by invasion from the south. In their zones of Greece and Yugoslavia, the Germans were plagued by attacks on small outposts and transportation lines, sapping their strength, tying down units and equipment urgently needed in the active theaters of war, and hampering the organization of an effective defense against Allied landings.

The German Offensive Against the Chetniks

From February 22, 1942, until May 14, 1943, Kolašin was a Chetnik stronghold and General Mihailović's headquarters for much of that time. But in May 1943 the German forces suddenly struck from Hercegovina on one side and Kosovo-Metohija on the other. Elite German units, including the famous Prinz Eugen SS division, inflicted heavy casualties on the Chetniks, capturing Maj. Pavle Djurišić with 4,000 men, and forcing Mihailović back into Serbia with the battered remnants of his command.

The southern flank of the German advance was guarded by the Albanian SS Division "Skenderbey"; the northern flank was covered by the Muslims from Sanjak. Both these sworn enemies of Montenegrin Serbs were finally free to give vent to their centuries-long, accumulated bitterness and hatred of the people of the unconquerable mountains. While the Germans themselves refrained from looting and destruction, they did nothing to stop their Muslim allies from indulging in an orgy of destructive violence against the Montenegrin Serbs. The worst hit were Serbian-Montenegrin communities around Bijelo Polje and in the area of Plav and Gusinje. The loot was spectacular: so many Montenegrin sheep were taken to Albanian-controlled territory around Peć that the 60-mile road from Kolašin to Peć was clogged by them for hours on end and, as German commanders complained, the animals hindered the passage of German units.

After his capture Pavle Djurišić was taken to the airport at Berane and, from there, by plane to the POW camp at Striy in western Ukraine. The rank and file were taken to camps in Germany, and some of them to labor camps in Salonika. It was only at this point that Germany finally decided to treat the members of the Royal Yugoslav Army in the Homeland as prisoners of war in accordance with the Geneva Convention.

The Chetnik war effort was seriously damaged by the heavy blow they received at the hands of the Germans in May. The Italians followed up their allies' advance and interned many local prominent Serbs, taking further hundreds to camps in Italy. Most surviving units had withdrawn to their native territories to become anticommunist militias that had no structure beyond the level of the clan and no strategic concept broader than defense of the village and local territory.

The Germans had learned from their experience in the Balkans and in Russia, and they set out to contain the guerillas and keep up the flow of bauxite and other strategic materials to the German war machine.[27] To protect their operations, they set up a network of *Tützpunkte* (strong points) to secure vital rail and road arteries and important installations. These strong points were actually small forts, heavily armed with automatic weapons, mortars, antitank guns, and even light field pieces.

A highly effective offensive weapon was found in the Jagdkommando (ranger detachment), designed to seek out and destroy guerrilla bands. These kommandos were usually young and combat-wise veterans, who had been trained to live in the open and off the land for extended periods of time. They were able to pursue the guerrillas, who had to move more slowly because they were taking with them not only their wounded, but families, and baggage.

By the end of 1943, British policy in the Balkans was increasingly under the influence of Communist agents and Communist sympathizers. James Klugman, the Communist mole at the Special Operations Executive in Cairo, was in the vital position of collecting signals from the Balkans and editing (or in Klugman's case, rewriting) them into reports that were transmitted to London. Klugman and his friends created a false picture of Mihailović, and under his influence (and from a general desire to be nice to Stalin), the British decided to abandon Mihailović and began withdrawing Allied liaison officers from the Chetniks. With their departure, the supply of weapons and equipment from the Middle East forces and Italy was reduced, much of it diverted to the Partisans.[28] The position of the Chetniks, who were under constant attack by Tito's forces, began to deteriorate rapidly. Though they still held Serbia and some of the Adriatic coastal regions, their strength was sapped by casualties and desertions.

Although Soviet agents like Guy Burgess did their best to undermine faith in Mihailović, who was accused of collaborating with the Germans, Tito's own deals with the Germans were either unknown or kept secret.[29] Although Mihailović's loyalty to the royal Yugoslavian Government-in-Exile could not be seriously questioned, there is ample evidence that a number of his subordinates made armistice arrangements with the occupation forces and even assisted them on occasion. Certain the Germans and their allies would eventually be forced to withdraw from the Balkans, Chetnik leaders saw a still-greater threat to the future of Yugoslavia in the Partisans, who were Moscow's advance guard for a communist revolution.

End Game

When Pavle Djurišić and 4,000 of his elite fighters were taken prisoner in May 1943, Tito's Partisans were the main beneficiaries. The Chetnik movement in Montenegro was suddenly decapitated, and in the crucial three months leading up to the capitulation of Italy, the Communists were gaining the upper hand. Another blow fell when groups led by General Djukanović and Col. Bajo Stanišić were slaughtered at Ostrog on October 15-18, 1943. Stanišić's group contained many noncommunist intellectuals, whom the communists regarded as an important target for elimination.

The Germans did not bother to keep Montenegro under permanent occupation. They were content to hold on to the coastline and to maintain a few garrisons important to their transport and communication network (Cetinje, Podgorica, Nikšić) with fortified points in between. They wisely relied on the Chetniks and Partisans to cripple the resistance efforts by slaughtering each other. Some places, including the ill-fated Kolašin, changed hands repeatedly, and each conquest and reconquest produced another round of killings so that the people who survived fell under suspicion for the mere fact that they had not been killed by the retreating enemy.

Three months after being taken prisoner, Maj. Pavle Djurišić managed to escape from the German POW camp at Striy. After a long ordeal, he reached the Danube near Pančevo, where he was captured (in October 1943) while trying to cross the Danube. Djurišić was taken to the Gestapo prison in Belgrade. Learning of his capture, General Nedić (the Serbian Pétain) intervened with the Germans to permit Djurišić to rejoin his Chetniks in Montenegro, on the understanding that he would not attack German units. Djurišić agreed, and in November 1943 he was once again in charge of his forces in Sanjak.

By that stage of the war, the Allies had decisively turned their back on Mihailović. Germany was obviously doomed, and—like many other Serbs squeezed between Churchill's rock and Tito's hard place—Djurišić chose the lesser of the two evils: to abandon the war against the Germans to be able to fight the communists. In the early spring of 1944, Djurišić was instrumental in preventing the breakthrough of Tito's forces from the northwestern part of Sanjak into Serbia, but in late April, heavily outnumbered by the Partisans, who were amply supplied by the Allies, Djurišić's forces suffered a setback at Mojkovac. They retreated to Sanjak and returned to Montenegro in June, when Chetnik formations were reconverted from local clan-based units to mobile formations that could engage in a broader struggle.

In August and September 1944, the Chetniks managed to withstand a determined attack by several crack Partisan divisions, but all this gallantry was in vain. Bad news came in, with the force of a rockslide: The first Soviet troops were arriving in Yugoslavia (at Kladovo, across the Danube from Rumania); the Western Allies finally revealed that were not going not to land in the Adriatic (according to Churchill they had never intended to—their threats were only a ruse to keep the Chetniks fighting); young King Petar, pressured by Britain and the United States, issued his September 12 proclamation effectively recognizing Tito as the only legitimate resistance leader. The total effect of these events meant that the Chetniks were completely lost.

The Chetniks had been intending to concentrate their forces in the coastal region. Following the anticipated German withdrawal, they hoped to hold on to a strip of free territory until the Allies arrived. If this scenario could not be played out, Djurišić planned to withdraw along the coastal plains of Albania to Greece. With this in mind, he established contact (in October) with the anticommunist resistance in Albania, whose leader Mark Gjon Markaja faced a similar predicament. Djurišić's forces also started preparing stockpiles of food and supplies, much of it left behind by the retreating Germans.

The Soviet offensive had already paved the road to power for Tito in Serbia itself: The Partisans, hiding behind Soviet tanks, entered Belgrade on October 20. Major Djurišić urged General Mihailović to withdraw to Montenegro, where he believed (on the advice of his quartermaster) that the Chetnik-held areas of Montenegro could support 100,000 soldiers for up to six months.

To Djurišić's chagrin, Mihailović changed his mind, and, after reaching Sjenica in Sanjak, he decided to retreat northwest to Bosnia rather than southwest to Montenegro. To put the finishing touch on the catastrophe, Mihailović ordered Djurišić to concentrate his forces, abandon Montenegro, and join him in Bosnia. The decision to go to Bosnia was, by all accounts, a major strategic blunder. What began as an orderly retreat turned into a rout, and in the bitter winter of 1945 the surviving Chetnik forces could not find sufficient supplies in Bosnian villages, which—dirt-poor at the outbreak of the war—had been burnt and looted so often that they could not provide fodder for a goat, much less for a company of soldiers.

Pavle Djurišić was under considerable pressure from his commanders and advisors not to obey Mihailović's order. He turned a deaf ear to their pleading, partly from a sense of military discipline and respect for the commander and partly because he believed that Draža had a game plan that he could not disclose by radio or even by courier. In January, the withdrawal was complete, and Djurišić's group that concentrated in Rudo (Bosnia) numbered some 17,000, of which about 4,000 were refugees and noncombatants (including all leading noncommunist intellectuals who had not been slaughtered, as well as Metropolitan Joanikije and 80 priests). On the Feast of St. John (January 20), Djurišić met with Chetnik commanders from Serbia, who explained the gravity of the situation including the betrayal of the so-called Allies. Mihailović, it was clear, had still not made up his mind whether to retreat further west toward Slovenia or to make a last stand in Bosnia. Nobody suspected at that time that he would opt for the worst of all worlds—an attempted breakthrough back to Serbia. On January 25-26, Montenegrin Chetniks had their first firefight with the Croatian Ustaša, and they found themselves pressed simultaneously by the Croats on one side and Tito's partisans on the other. This was the first omen of the fatal train of events that was to follow.

The prospect of a further retreat through Bosnia was terrible: The Chetniks and their dependents were weak and poorly clothed (especially those from the coastal areas); food was scarce, and they were running out of ammunition and supplies. To make things worse, typhoid fever was taking its toll. Djurišić realized he could no longer remain in central Bosnia with a commander who could offer no clear objective and no prospect of improvement. In late March, Djurišić received two emissaries sent by Sekula Drljević, who had come from Zagreb to plead with him to "save the people" by withdrawing across northern Bosnia and central Croatia (both held by the Ustaša) to Slovenia. They brought a letter with Drljević's pledge and word of honor that the Croatian authorities would let them pass unhindered if they promised to make the trip in peace.

Djurišić could not have trusted the promise of the man he and every other honorable Montenegrin despised, even before he had signed on as Ante Pavelić's paid agent, but he felt he had little choice. The result could have been predicted. Massive Ustaša forces, some of them withdrawn from the front in Srem and the Drava valley, where they were facing the Red Army, suddenly attacked Djurišić's column in the area of Lijevča Polje in northwest Bosnia. The

Metropolitan Joanikije Lipovac

Croats, supplied with tanks and artillery, ambushed Djurišić's forces, and though the battle (April 4-7) was hard-fought, Djurišić's exhausted army—outnumbered and outgunned—was, in the end, defeated.[30]

Of the 17,000 troops that had gathered at Rudo four months earlier, 5,000 survived to be taken prisoner and escorted by the Ustaše to the old Austrian fort and prison in Stara Gradiška, on the northern (Croatian) side of the Sava. Sekula Drljević and his followers then picked out, one by one as they filed by, 120 officers and noncombatant intellectuals, who were taken by the Ustaše to the Sava River late at night on April 20, 1945. They were loaded onto boats and never seen again. Some say they were taken to nearby Jasenovac (the infamous death camp) and killed there, while others say that they were slaughtered in a marsh on the Bosnian side of the Sava.

Leaderless and demoralized, the surviving Chetniks were assembled on April 21 at Gradiška, where they were addressed by Sekula Drljević, who told them they had been misled. Now they were to be "the army of Montenegro," and he was their leader. Drljević ordered them to take off their Chetnik insignia and to put on badges of his own design that had been made in Zagreb—another proof, as if any were needed, that the ambush at Lijevča Polje had been premeditated by Pavelić and his stooge. Drljević marched his "army" to Slovenia, but as soon as they left the territory of Pavelić's Croatia, the Montenegrins threw away the made-in-Zagreb badges of Montenegrin nationalism and put their Chetnik insignia back on. The deluded and now disappointed Drljević had to drive away with his armed Ustaša escort, never to see his "army" again. Three of his subordinates were killed soon after by their enraged compatriots. Later in 1945 Drljević was executed in Austria by two survivors from Djurišić's group, who maintained their Montenegrin sense of justice.

The remnant of surviving patriotic Serbs might have thought their ordeal was finally over when they surrendered to the British near Klagenfut in the first week of May 1945. Little did they suspect that, two weeks later, they would be put on trains, which they were told would transport them to Italy, and delivered to Tito's executioners. A scant 500 survived by hiding from the British, or otherwise evading capture—roughly one in 34 from the original 17,000.[31]

Notes

Good summaries of Yugoslav history from 1918 to 1945 are given by Lampe and (despite the Titoist propaganda obligatory during the period) by Dedijer *et al.* Djilas's *Wartime* is a brilliant though one-sided personal description of the Partisans.

1. See Dragnich, *Serbs and Croats.*

2. Although the name Yugoslavia was only adopted later, it was in colloquial use from the beginning.

3. See discussion in Petrovitch, vol. II.

4. For regional and ethnic separatisms in Europe and America, see Fleming "A League of Our Own" and "American Crack-up."

5. Trifković, *Ustaša.*

6. Djilas, Land, pp. 89-93.

7. Ivo Banac, pp. 270-91.

8. Drljević, *Balkanski sukobi.*

9. These ethnic fictions were to take on renewed and deadly force when foreign journalists like Noel Malcolm and Tim Judah were enlisted to compose their justifications for the U.S.-NATO attacks on Yugoslavia.

10. Pilar's and Štedimlija's creative race-theories on the Croat origins of the Montenegrins were refuted long ago by the prominent Croatian historian Ferdo Šišic, who explored the same period in his seminal *Povijest Hrvata* (*History of the Croats*, (Zagreb, 1925). Šišic insisted that "the occasional presence of the Croat name in the 11th and 12th century in Upper Dalmatia still does not mean that the area was part of Croatia, or even that we are dealing with ethnic Croats. It only means that among the Serbs of Doclea there have been groups known as Croats, just as we encounter such groups among the Czechs and Poles in the tenth and eleventh century." For a discussion of the "ideological roots of Montenegrin . . . separatism," see Slavenko Terzić, Director of the Historical Institute of the Serbian Academy of Sciences and Arts, on *www.Njegos.org.*

11. Bataković, "Ujedinjenje."

12. Pešić, p. 262.

13. For negotiations leading to the signing of the pact, see Hoptner.

14. Trifković, "Prince Pavle."

15. Terzić, *Aprilski rat.*

16. Redžić, p. 23.

17. Djilas, *Wartime*, pp. 49ff.; cf. West, *Tito*, pp. 103-02.

18. Minić, *Rasute kosti*, p. 123.

19. See Redžić for a comprehensive survey of documentary sources and personal accounts of the Kolašin affair.

20. Minić, p. 127.

21. Vojnoistorijski institut Jugoslavije: Zbornik dokumenata, NOB, I-4, 1954, p. 123.

22. *Op. cit.* III-2, 1950, pp. 210-211, and II-3, 1955, p. 97.

23. Walter Roberts, pp. 79-81.

24. Trifković (1998), pp. 185-90.

25. A moving account of an Italian officer in Yugoslavia arrested by the Germans after the fall of Musolini is given by Giuseppe Podesta (1990).

26. This was confirmed by Guido Lucich-Rocchi to Stevan Pavlowitch (according to his student, Srdja Trifković). Lucich-Rocchi was an Italian officer who spoke Serbian fluently and served in Knin and Split during the war. The command of the Second Army was very Anglophile and hoped for a link with Mihailović and the British through their Serb "nationalists." The same impression was shared by General Umberto Salvatores who, then still a colonel, commanded the 6th Bersaglieri Regiment in Lika and Bosnia.

27. For a description of German tactics in Yugoslavia, see Hehn.

28. See David Martin.

29. Roberts, pp. 106-112.

30. Predrag Čemović provides a detailed eye-witness account: "Od Podgorice do Gradiške," *Glasnik društva "Njegoš,"* Vol. VII (June 1961), pp. 45-88.

31. For an accurate, though controversial, account, see Nikolai Tolstoy.

THE SECOND (AND THIRD) YUGOSLAVIAS

A time for "settling scores" is the phrase most commonly used to describe the aftermath of the World War II in Yugoslavia, but it is hard to imagine a more perverse characterization of the period. Long before the war, the Yugoslav Communists knew that to establish a Communist state would require the murder of hundreds of thousands of people: rich businessmen, of course, but also peasants who owned a few acres, convinced royalists as well as Marxists who had not joined Stalin's party, to say nothing of priests, civil servants, and anyone who displayed the slightest capacity for independent thought. The Italian occupation of Montenegro and the subsequent uprising gave Communists the opportunity to begin the massacre under the cover of wartime exigency, and by the end of the war, they and the Ustaša had gone a long way toward purging Montenegro (and the whole Serbian nation) of "reactionary elements," though there were still a few survivors to be dealt with.

As Tito explained to Aleksandar Ranković, the few remaining Chetniks had to be hunted down (and exterminated) "to strike terror into the hearts of those who did not like this sort of Yugoslavia." To drive their message of terror home, the Communists killed about 100,000 people after the end of the war. Perhaps no more than one percent of that number were in Montenegro, mainly because most of the people slated for killing had already been dispatched to one "Dog Cemetery" or another, or hurled into a mountain crevice, or killed fighting Italians, Germans, Muslims, Albanians, or Communists. Some were among the remnant who perished on Pavle Djurišić's doomed retreat.

Well aware of what was in store for them when Tito's forces arrived, many surviving "nationalists" joined the Partizani or else left with the retreating Germans. As Partisan units entered Cetinje, Podgorica, Nikšić, and the Littoral in November 1944, the only remaining inhabitants were people who had assumed that they had nothing to hide and nothing to fear.

They were swiftly disabused. In the first 24 hours after entering Cetinje on November 13, the Partisans arrested 28 citizens and summarily shot them at Humci, Cetinje's "New Cemetery." The most prominent of them was Professor Ilija Zorić, director of the Cetinje Lyceum (*Gimnazija*). Zorić was a prominent historian who had also gained considerable respect between two world wars for his literary criticism and his work for the Cetinje Theater.[1]

None of the victims had been in any way politically active. Aleksandra Matanović was a completely apolitical young woman of 27. She had completed her studies of the English language and literature in Belgrade on the eve of the war. Perhaps her education was reason enough to shoot her, though it is hard to imagine a rational motive for shooting a 17-year-old high-school student who was executed along with the others. Perhaps he got good grades. Five of those killed had taught at the Lyceum, another four were civil or municipal servants (including a popular prewar mayor of the city), and 12 others were university graduates—still a rarity in Montenegro at that time. It was obvious that the executions, in addition to striking terror into the people, fit the desire of Communist revolutionaries everywhere to exterminate intellectuals and "community leaders" as such, regardless of what they did, said, or thought. In fact, the elimination of the fittest is an ancient device of tyranny well known to Herodotus and Aristotle.

Unlike most Communist executioners, who were reluctant to come clean about their crimes, Tito's "Hero of the People" and retired general Blažo Janković talked about this period to the Montenegrin daily *Pobjeda* (March 10, 1992). He readily acknowledged that the victims of the "liberators" were totally innocent and "explained" that the inclusion of so many teachers among them may have been due to the desire for revenge nurtured by some of his comrades who had not done well at school. Such people were the masters of life and death in Montenegro after November 1944.

World War II was an unmitigated disaster for Montenegro, far worse than any Turkish punitive expedition of the previous four centuries. Of approximately 400,000 people, close to 55,000 were dead.[2] Of just over 100,000 able-bodied males, almost one half had lost their lives, making Montenegro proportionately the most blood-soaked spot in Europe. More significantly still, among the patriotic Serbs, men in their prime, soldiers, scholars, priests, prosperous and hardworking farmers, who had provided the backbone to their communities and to the Montenegrin society, the loss approached 100 percent. The term "genocide" has been discredited by overuse and political manipulation, but there is no better word to

describe the fate of Montenegrins. Small wonder that Communists assumed that they could create a new identity and invent a new history for
the devastated land filled with women in black.

The New Yugoslavia

In the years leading up to the war, the Communist Party had repudiated Yugoslavia, describing it as a means of oppressing ethnic minorities.
The party line switched abruptly in the late 1930's, when Hitler was in
the Rhineland and the Popular Front held power in Paris. In the end,
however, Tito decided upon a unified state in the form of a federal republic, whose federalism was as fictitious as the "Union" of Soviet Socialist
Republics. A true federal union, such as the original Swiss and American
republics, is based on a voluntary pact among sovereign (or semi-
sovereign) states. Authority is not delegated from the top to the lower lev-
els of government, but radiates upward from the roots.[3] The Communist
government of Yugoslavia might insert all the federalist language it liked
into the various constitutions it concocted every few years, but none of
this Constitutional rhetoric could alter the reality of a centralized party
state designed to serve the interests of the leader and his principal supporters. There was absolutely nothing egalitarian about such a society.
The system of Communist exploitation was first described by the Montenegrin Communist Milovan Djilas in his book *The New Class*, in which
he observed that Communists eliminate every form of property except
their own.

Despite some pressure from Stalin to form a larger Yugoslavia that
would include Albania and perhaps Bulgaria, the borders of the new Yugoslavia were not much different from those of the kingdom. The new
Communist government (the pathetic fiction of a multi-party democracy
was soon abandoned) established separate republics of Croatia, Slovenia,
Serbia, Macedonia, Bosnia-Hercegovina, and Montenegro. The Communists drew up the borders of these "federal republics" as if their goal were
to create the ethnic confusion that only the strong hand of the leader
could control.

The more important goal, however, was the dampening of Serb nationalism. This was accomplished in several ways. First, many Serbs were
included in Croatia and Bosnia, and when the breakup came in the
1990's, these extraterritorial Serbs were threatened by militantly anti-Serb
governments. Secondly, two autonomous regions were established as

part of Serbia: Vojvodina, where a Serb majority coexisted with Hungarians, Slovaks, and Germans (most of whom were expelled after 1945); and Kosovo, where a Serb minority was subject to constant harassment by Albanians, whose ambition to live in a Serb-free land was encouraged first by the Turks, then by the Nazis, then by the Communists, and finally realized at the end of the NATO attack on Yugoslavia. Thirdly, Montenegrins were given their own republic and encouraged to alienate themselves from other Serbs.

The confusing boundaries of these multiethnic republics, when combined with Yugoslavist ideology and the emerging theory of Montenegrin nationalism, provided the perfect formula to keep ethnic questions simmering and to ensure the need for Tito's strong ruling hand to mediate among the party oligarchies that represented the different components of the multiethnic state. How much of this was calculated from the beginning and how much was merely the *ad hoc* adjustments of stupid and self-seeking politicians remains to be seen. What is certain is that neither of Tito's principal lieutenants, Kardelj and Ranković, displayed the slightest talent for rebuilding a nation, managing an economy, or writing a constitution.

Before they were through, the Yugoslav constitution would be second in length only to India's, taking up such crucial questions as workers' self-management, veterans' pensions, and the distribution of socially owned apartments. The first Communist constitution did, however, hold out the possibility that the republics might secede. The 1953 revision, however, eliminated that possibility, and sovereignty, which had been vested in the republics, belonged to the people, or rather, to the Communist Party. The competing ethnic nationalisms, it was hoped, would be replaced by the noble concept of *Jugoslovenstvo* ("Yugoslavism").

Like the constitution of 1946, the 1953 document created more problems than it solved, especially in the economic sector. The 1963 constitution, drafted as usual by Kardelj, was designed to facilitate economic reforms and to keep the separate republics and ethnic interests as isolated as possible.[4]

The previous emphasis on Yugoslavism had allowed the unpleasant possibility (if only in theory) of unified opposition to the central state, and to meet that threat the new constitution appeared to delegate considerable powers to the republics and regions. Even the possibility of secession, which had been eliminated in 1953, was restored, and a new court was set up to rule on claims that a republic's rights were being infringed by the central government.

Predictably, the new constitution raised the expectations of Slovenes and Croats, and Croatian intellectuals, led by Miroslav Krleža, were openly complaining of discrimination against their traditions in the late 1960's. Krleža was a classic example of the self-serving political intellectual: He was a known Communist, albeit one who was guilty of "factionalism" in the 1930's; he sat out World War II in Croatia for reasons of "health" without being molested by Pavelić's government. After the war, Krleža's friendship with Tito shielded him from the consequences of his live-and-let-live relations with the Ustaša and gave him the opportunity to cultivate his vision of Mitteleuropean Croatia with the same impunity he enjoyed as a Communist in wartime Croatia.

In 1971, a series of constitutional amendments increased the powers of the republics, and in the incredibly complicated 1974 constitution, representatives to the Chamber of Republics and Autonomous Provinces were supposed to vote under the direction of their home assemblies. With its cumbersome apparatus of indirect elections, the new system ensured that all political figures (with one significant exception) would be virtual nonentities that no one in the general public had ever heard of and answerable to party oligarchs.[5]

After Tito's death in 1980, the clumsy system limped along for a decade, powerless to stem the upsurge of ethnic nationalisms. By the mid-1980's, Yugoslavia was in the throes of an economic and political crisis that the old guard Titoists were unable to contain. New leaders, eager to capitalize on national resentments, began to emerge: the careerist Communist Milan Kučan in Slovenia and, in Croatia, the dissident Franjo Tudjman, who had been one of Tito's generals but later fell into disgrace for his nationalism. In Serbia, Ivan Stambolić, head of Serbia's League of Communists, had begun to warn against the Communist strategy of suppressing the Serbs and went so far as to criticize the continued demonization of the Chetniks. Stambolić was arguing not in favor of Serb nationalism, but—on the contrary—against anti-Serb nationalisms. However, his protégé, Slobodan Milošević, emerged as the undisputed boss in Serbia at the eighth session of the republic's League of Communists Central Committee meeting in September 1987. Milošević courted popularity in Serbia by denouncing the Albanian persecution of Serbs in Kosovo and by portraying himself as the defender of Serbs, a mantle that set very clumsily on the shoulders of a Marxist opportunist.

Yugoslavia was coming apart at the seams, whoever was, the Serbian party boss, but Milošević's rhetoric may have helped to precipitate the crisis in 1991, when Slovenian, Croatian, and Bosnian Muslim political leaders, whose dreams of independence were encouraged by government disarray after Tito's death, decided that they could play the nationalist card as well as Milošević. Although the Macedonian election in December 1990 brought to power a "reform" Communist government in favor of union, Kiro Grigorov was unwilling to share the growing international hostility to the Milošević regime, and in September 1991, after a referendum, Macedonia declared its independence. Only Milošević's Montenegrin lieutenants, like Momir Bulatović, stayed loyal.

Montenegro

Montenegro virtually disappears from view in the Tito years. The tiniest republic had one role to play, and a passive one at that: Stay divided from Serbia and develop a sense of nationhood that would be the cause of a permanent division. The "Montenegrin nation" was a concept that had to be imposed gradually, step by step after 1945. In the beginning, the Communist slogan was, "We are both Serbs and Montenegrins," and as Tito's Communist regime proclaimed in 1945: "Montenegrins are different Serbs from other Serbs." Already by 1948, the Party's Montenegrin nationalism was taking on anti-Serbian tones, which violated the spirit of the officially proclaimed proletarian internationalism. This was a pardonable mistake, however, and throughout the Communist period it would have been political suicide for someone to proclaim himself as anything but "Montenegrin" (let alone as a Serb).

There is little to be said about events in Titoist Montenegro, because little or nothing actually happened. Communism is a repressive, not a creative, force. Cuba, after being taken over by Fidel Castro, experienced sugar shortages, and there is an old joke about a possible Soviet threat to North Africa. "What would happen," asks a French statesmen, "if Communists took over the Sahara desert?" "Nothing for the first five years," he is told, "and then there would be a sand shortage." Montenegro entered the Communist phase as one of the poorest regions in Europe, and Montenegro remained desperately poor, despite the Potemkin Village projects designed to enhance the regime's prestige: Two international airports (at Tivat and Podgorica) were built at a distance of only 60 miles; the steelworks constructed at Nikšić had to import iron ore and scrap metal from hundreds, even thousands of miles away; the aluminum plant at Podgorica—an eyesore and an environmental catastrophe—faced similar problems, while the ugly tourist hotels which dotted the historic coastline were poorly built and worse maintained.

Ordinary Montenegrins learned how to survive the new occupation as they had survived the more benign rule of the Turks. But like the Turks, the Communists levied a blood tax on Montenegrin children, who were brought up to repudiate their heritage and inform on their parents, who were naturally reluctant to talk about history and tradition in the presence of brainwashed children. A history dealing with public life in Montenegro offers the disagreeable spectacle of petty Communist bosses, outdoing each other in servility to the leader and squabbling over booty that a crooked small-town alderman in America would scorn. The top bosses, in search for richer prizes, moved to Belgrade. As the postwar joke put it, Cetinje descended to Dedinje (a fashionable Belgrade suburb). When two Montenegrin veterans of the Partisans met on the street, so the story goes, they did not greet each other with the usual "What are you doing?" (*Šta radiš?*) but "Where are you managing?" (*Gdje rukovodiš?*). After 500 years of heroic struggles, Communist Montenegro was decidedly an anticlimax.

Montenegrin Communists did, however, face a number of critical conflicts of loyalty that would have been difficult to imagine in the heady days at the end of the war. Tito's break with Stalin in 1948 caused the fall of "Panslavist" Montenegrins, who were rabid in their loyalty to Russia. Arso Jovanović, the Montenegrin Partisan general so beloved by his comrades, was caught trying to escape to Rumania and shot. Of the 60,000 members imprisoned for "Cominformism" (that is, loyalty to the U.S.S.R.), 20 percent were Montenegrin, though Montenegrins accounted for only 2.5 percent of the population. The cruelties practiced on Goli Otok (The Barren Island) fully matched the savagery of the Gulag set up by the pro-Russian Communists' idol in Moscow.

The few surviving Montenegrin Communists who remained true to their ideals faced a second, though less severe problem in 1954, when Milovan Djilas, the only Montenegrin in Tito's inner circle, was denounced and dismissed from the Central Committee. Djilas had been the only original mind in the Yugoslav Communist Party, and the Party's shift (in the early 1950's) to more liberal policies was largely his inspiration. But admiration and celebrity come at a price in a society devoted to the worship of the leader. Seeing the applause given to her son at the

Sixth Party Congress in 1952, his worried mother remarked, "It is not good for our Djido, when he receives more applause than Tito." On an earlier occasion (so the story is told), when the crowd in Podgorica gave their Communist favorite son a thundering ovation, Djilas noticed the look on Tito's face and, in a brilliant piece of political improvisation, immediately proposed that Podgorica be renamed Titograd.

After turning in his CPY membership card, Djilas was later to spend years in jail for the criticism he published of Titoist Yugoslavia and of the Communist system as a whole. Although a brilliant man, Djilas remained loyal to Marxist ideals almost until the end, and he never strayed much farther from the reservation than into the left-wing socialism of the British Labour Party. Although only Vladimir Dedijer (Tito's official biographer) and his first wife stood by him personally (they repudiated his views), Djilas in disgrace became something of a liability to some of his former friends. In fact, Montenegrin Communists never really recovered from the double blow, and after Djilas's fall, none of them held a key position among Tito's top leadership.

As time went on, the old comrade became the center of a group of dissident writers such as Matija Bećković, Mihajlo Mihajlov, Dragoljub Ignjatović, and Momčilo Selić. To make matters worse, some of them had been brought up as the privileged children of the party. To show what a small world it was, you only have to consider the fact that the dissident Selić was not only the son of Partisan parents but was married to the daughter of a leading politician and, through his wife who was half-sister to Mira Marković, Slobodan Milošević's brother-in-law. For their writings (some of it published in the journal *Časovnik*), Mihajlov and Selić would serve prison terms for defaming the leader or the system he created. The contradictions in Djilas's thought are reflected in the future careers of two of his collaborators. While Mihajlov, who was of Russian parentage, went on to be a spokesman for democratic human rights, labor unions, and all the other causes championed by social democrats, Selić, a Montenegrin who wrote more powerful narrative fiction than Djilas, turned eventually to Serb nationalism and the Orthodox Church. If Mihajlov reflected the master's mind, Selić revealed his soul.

The "Real Montenegro"

In repressing the spirit of Serb patriotism, however, the Communists were not content merely to play with the map and promote Yugoslav unity. They also picked up the Austrian game of inventing nations. During the Tito years, Montenegrin students were subjected to a propaganda barrage, whose materials were drawn from Croatian propagandists and their Montenegrin imitators, to make them believe in a separate Montenegrin nation. Štedimlija's spirit permeated the school curricula, academic textbooks, popular culture, and political forums, while allusions to the common traditions of the Serbs were simply not permitted. The cadres for the project were recruited from among the thousands of Montenegrin students who, between 1946 and 1966, were deliberately sent to the University of Zagreb for this purpose.

The ostensible triumph of Croatia in the wars of Yugoslav succession and the parallel demonization of the Serbs in the West have given heart to the heirs of Pilar, Štedimlija and Drljević, Krleža, Pavelić and Tito himself. The new Montenegrin nationalists went far beyond Štedimlija, who had to "explain" things that were obviously false. His heirs have relied on six decades of officially sanctioned lies, state indoctrination, and police terror that erased the historical record and implanted into its victims a false memory of a nonexistent nationality. In this new world, which might have been designed by the science-fiction writer Philip K. Dick, people no longer knew that, in 1945, there were no other "Montenegrins" than Serbs. By the 1990's, the products of this massive experiment in social engineering were ready to convert Štedimlija's fantasy of Montenegro as a Western colony into reality.

The symbolic triumph of this cabal came in 1972, the year of Kardelj's constitution, with the demolition of the mausoleum chapel built by Prince-Bishop Petar II Petrović Njegoš in 1845-46 on Mt. Lovćen. In August 1916, the Austrian-Hungarian occupation forces destroyed the Njegoš Chapel, intending to build a monument to the Dual Monarchy, but it was rebuilt in September 1925 by King Aleksandar Karadjordjević. The anti-Serb separatists thought they scored a major victory when the chapel was razed to the ground (illegally, since the chapel had always been Church property) and replaced in 1974 with an ugly neo-pagan edifice filled with Masonic symbolism—designed by the Croat sculptor, Ivan Meštrović—that is now known as the Njegoš Mausoleum. In another symbolic act, one even more fraught with future consequences, the remains of King Nikola Petrović were brought back to Cetinje in 1989.

Support for Montenegrin independence was not a uniform phenomenon. Albanians and Sanjak Muslims obviously saw Montenegrin independence as the first step toward gaining their own objectives: inde-

Chapel of Petar II Petrović Njegoš

pendence or unification with Albania or Islamic Bosnia. Many people were quite naturally disgusted with Milošević, who had made Yugoslavia a pariah state, subject to sanctions and a target for NATO attacks. However, every political movement is ultimately directed by its radical elements, and even decent and patriotic Montenegrin Serbs were slowly brainwashed into an ambivalent attitude toward their heritage. The separatist ideology was crafted by the so-called Duklja Academy of Sciences and Arts (DANU), whose chairman, Jevrem Brković, was a good example of the Montenegrin revisionists who thought that in building a "new" Montenegro, it was necessary to jettison not just the Serbian heritage but even the legacy of the Petrović Njegoš dynasty.[6] Despite the barrage of pseudo-academic propaganda, most Montenegrin Serbs continued to oppose secession. Their almost atavistic patriotism was troublesome to the international community. "The trouble is that so many Montenegrins still mistakenly imagine that they are Serbs," a German analyst explained with surprising frankness in a Radio Free Europe interview (June 2000).

The Third Yugoslavia

In the early days of the wars of Yugoslav succession, Montenegro was kept loyal to the Belgrade government by Milošević's loyal lieutenant, Momir Bulatović, another "reform" Communist who had (as they say in Serbia) "turned his coat inside-out." He had been elected to the Montenegrin legislature in 1988 on Milošević's slogan of the "anti-bureaucratic revolution" and quickly took over the Montenegrin government with the help of his ally, Milo Djukanović, becoming first the secretary of the

Central Committee, then the founder (with Djukanović again) of the Democratic Party of Socialists (DPS), and (in 1993) president of Montenegro. In 1992 Bulatović, once again backed by Djukanović (whom he had made his prime minister), managed the referendum on separation and rallied Montenegrins to the slogan "Yugoslavia without an alternative." But even as early as 1992, Dobrica Ćosić (novelist and federal president) was warning both Bulatović and Djukanović that it was time to slip out from under the AVNOJ yoke that Milošević had fastened around his country's neck. "Look, boys," he is supposed to have told the young politicos, as Montenegrins they would be listened to as prophets here in Belgrade, if they espoused an authentic Serbian nationalism. Bulatović seemed uncomprehending, but Djukanović smiled at the prospect of making himself a national leader.[7]

Sanctions imposed on Yugoslavia made the Milošević regime and its supporters less and less popular in Montenegro. By 1995, Djukanović began to criticize Milošević for his blunders in handling the negotiations for the Dayton Accords, and the next year he went into open conflict when Milošević refused to recognize the results of Serbian elections that gave victory to his opponents. In 1997, with nowhere else to go, the ex-Communist/Serb nationalist Djukanović reinvented himself — with the West's encouragement — as the exponent of Montenegrin national identity. Capitalizing on Milošević's unpopularity (and total lack of a strategy), he made himself party leader of the DPS. Driving Bulatović out of the party, he got himself elected president of Montenegro, beating Bulatović (who had founded a new party) by a narrow margin, though the election was widely denounced as fraudulent.

Openly at odds with Milošević, Djukanović turned increasingly to the West, which welcomed him with open arms and used him as a tool for subjugating Yugoslavia. "I began meeting with Djukanović regularly, even before he became the president of Montenegro a year and a half ago," testified Robert Gelbard in the United States Senate on the "Prospects for Democratization in Yugoslavia," adding:

I was with him during his inauguration when we felt that a strong international presence, a public presence, would deter a Milošević-inspired coup. The U.S. provided $20 million in budgetary support over the last several months, when no other countries stepped in to fill the gap, and we're prepared to do more . . . While it [i.e. Montenegro] is too small to challenge Serbia directly, it can serve as a guiding light for the Serbian opposition. What Montenegro needs now is support from their European neighbors in concrete terms.[8]

Gelbard's candid avowal of monetary support lends some credence to Bulatović's charge that Gelbard had offered him a personal bribe of several million dollars. According to the British Helsinki Human Rights Group (April 2001), Montenegro, between 1997 and April 2001, received "millions of dollars in international aid and the US Congress has earmarked another large tranche of funds for the coming year. Much of his aid is used to pay salaries and pensions. By doing this the government in Podgorica was able to distance itself from cash-strapped Belgrade."

Milošević, who wanted to punish Djukanović for allying himself with Yugoslavia's NATO enemies, imposed a blockade on Montenegro. This only encouraged Djukanović in his program to make his small country increasingly self-sufficient and independent. The Yugoslav army (VJ) was still in Montenegro, and the federal government controlled the airspace, but Djukanović built up an enormous police force as an alternative to the army, and before long Montenegro was subject to jurisdictional conflicts between the federal army and the republic's paramilitary police. In May 1998, President Djukanović strengthened his political grip on the country, and his coalition "To Live Better" (which sounds like an ad slogan for a soft drink) gained 50 percent of the votes as opposed to Bulatović's new party, the Socialist People's Party (SNP), which received 35 percent.

To compensate Bulatović, who had lost his political base in Montenegro, Milošević named him federal prime minister, a move that further alienated Djukanović, who commented darkly:[9] "If anyone wants violence in Montenegro, he should know what to expect." In fact, there was rioting in Podgorica for three days leading up to Djukanović's inauguration on January 15, 1998. Eighteen months later, the Montenegrin president announced his refusal to acknowledge the constitutional legitimacy of Milošević's government and called upon Montenegrins to boycott the elections held in September. This enraged the leaders of the anti-Milošević coalition in Belgrade, who pointed out that the abstention of Montenegrin voters played into Milošević's hands.

The ever-faithful Momir Bulatović supported Milošević, calling his ultimately victorious rival, Vojislav Koštunica, "NATO's lackey." It would not be too long before Bulatović was ditched, and his party would be working, at least pragmatically, in a coalition with the "lackeys." Bulatović

worked hard to bring in 180,000 votes for the boss, and the votes were ver-
ified in advance by his party's leaders.[10] By this time Djukanović, apparently warned (by the Americans) against cooperating with the new Yugoslav government, was openly advocating independence, and though
his coalition came up with a disappointing 42 percent in the 2001 elections, he continued to campaign for separation.

Montenegrin Futures

Djukanović appeared to have staked his future on hostility to Milošević, both in Montenegro and in the "international community," but Koštunica's victory and, six months later, his mediocre showing in the Montenegrin election (April 2001) were a major setback for the governing
coalition, whose campaign was overwhelmingly focused on the issue of
total independence from the Yugoslav federation. The ruling coalition's
42 percent of the votes, as opposed to the 43 percent of parliamentary
mandates and 46 percent of the popular vote for the alliance supporting
continued union with Serbia, was not so much a "slim victory" as a
crushing defeat for Djukanović, whose ruling DPS and its ally, the
strongly separatist Social Democratic Party, had all the key media outlets
under their total control. The iron grip of the DPS on state television was
reminiscent of Serbia under Milošević, and with similar unintended results: Instead of being indoctrinated into separatist fervor, many Montenegrins were irritated by the stream of relentless propaganda passing
for the evening news bulletin.

"It couldn't be otherwise," a journalist from Cetinje commented,
"since Djukanović doesn't know how to be subtle. He is Milošević's disciple, his creation. He may parade as a democrat now, but his instincts
have always been authoritarian and remain so today." The leading daily
newspaper, *Pobjeda*, is controlled by the government and accordingly
looks and reads like a party organ from pre-1989 Eastern Europe. The
second-largest circulation daily, *Vijesti*, and the leading weekly, *Monitor*,
while theoretically "independent," are outspoken in their support of separatism and the Djukanović regime. Like many other press organs in the
Balkans, both support and encouragement from the foreign and international interests (*e.g.*, George Soros, the National Endowment for Democracy) whose views they echo.

Milošević's departure, however, has deprived Djukanović of one of
his principal attractions for NATO governments eager to bring about the

fall of the Serbian Strongman. In the spring of 2001, the Western media finally started reporting that the supporters of separatist candidates had engaged in systematic gerrymandering, with government officials exerting pressure on state employees (including over 20,000 policemen, in a land of 600,000 people!) to vote "the right way."

Tiit Kabin, special OSCE coordinator for the Montenegrin elections, while commenting favorably on the progress made toward clean elections, did confirm that there had been cases of pressure and police involvement in campaign activities. Other observers noted that some known opponents of the regime were denied the vote by not being included in the electoral roll, while many reliable supporters of the government apparently followed the old rule "vote early — vote often." The last-minute removal of ten percent of eligible voters from the rolls raised even more serious questions.[11]

Back to Illyria

In addition, Djukanović and his separatist allies could rely on considerable financial resources of a government structure in which the line between state and party funds is blurred at best. The European press has reported on a network of institutionalized corruption that has given Montenegro the reputation for being the smuggling capital of Europe. Such an apparatus could easily provide support for a government propaganda machine reminiscent of Milošević's. As the London *Independent* (April 24, 2001) observed of the Montenegrin leader,

> his critics as well as many ordinary Montenegrins say that he bears many resemblances to . . . Milošević. On matters of style, there is little obvious similarity: Mr. Djukanović is said to favour Armani suits and silk ties, but he controls the 20,000-strong police force, keeps control of the customs service and is alleged to have a key role in the lucrative cigarette smuggling trade.

The deals with major tobacco companies were set up by a Croatian partner.[12]

Montenegro, according to critics of the government, was turning into a Mafia resort community. Every evening, at around seven o'clock, powerful, long speedboats, loaded with cigarettes, leave the Montenegrin port of Bar. Under the cover of dark, the boats make the three-hour crossing to the Italian coast and land somewhere between Bari and Brindisi, where they are met by young men who hastily unload the cargo worth 450,000 German marks. The cigarette cartons are reloaded onto the trucks, which are escorted by half a dozen armored jeeps that take the cigarettes either to the Sacra Corona, the most powerful Mafia organization in Puglia, or to the Camorra in Naples.

According to Italian sources, Montenegro earns up to 60 percent of its domestic product from this "transit business," as it is known locally. The Italian state loses billions of lire a year in unpaid taxes, and other E.U. countries may soon be facing a similar loss of tax revenue. Montenegrin politicians avoid talking about the smuggling allegations, though Djukanović did denounce the Italian Finance Minister on the eve of the April 2001 elections. When forced to justify their actions, they point out that the practice went on for decades in the former Yugoslavia, out of Croatia, and that if Montenegro was to clamp down on the trade, another Balkan country would rapidly step in. Although the trade itself is not new, the attention it is receiving in Italy at present is unprecedented. The Italian finance minister, Ottaviano Del Turco, has already indicated that Djukanović would be arrested if he were bold enough to step on Italy's soil. The Zagreb weekly *Nacional* published a detailed expose that obviously relied in substantial part on information supplied by certain Western intelligence agencies.

In the summer of 2001, the Montenegrin government did announce a planned crackdown on corruption, but as an analyst from Podgorica's Center for Democracy pointed out, "It is difficult to imagine that the government will cleanse its own ranks of those implicated in corruption."[13]

Secession

Montenegrin politics in the first year of the new millennium (2001) were dominated by the separatists' demand for a referendum on secession. While the ultra-separatist Liberal Party and Djukanović's coalition insisted that a simple majority of those voting could decide the issue, opponents (including Yugoslav President Vojislav Koštunica)[14] pointed out that the complex provisions for amending the Montenegrin constitution required a two-thirds parliamentary vote before the issue could be submitted to the people. They also insisted that Montenegrin citizens residing in other parts of Yugoslavia be allowed to vote and, since they were threatening to boycott the referendum, that secession could not be decided by a vote of less than 50 percent of eligible voters. The separatists, who knew that they could not hope to win if they played by the rules, rejected all these stipulations.

Djukanović had been an astute politician, but by early 2002, he was trying to steer an avalanche going over a cliff. Pushed from behind by ultra-separatists (especially in the Liberalni Savez), who never fully believed his commitment to independence, he was less and less actively supported by the United States and its allies. Some of the Europeans might have been disgusted with the level of criminal activity apparently tolerated within Montenegro; the Americans began to lose interest after the fall of Milošević. Some sort of change may have been signaled when both the European Union and the U.S. ambassador to Belgrade began making noises about the need for a legitimate referendum.

Complicating the situation was the desire of both Serbia and Montenegro to begin the process of integration into the European Union. In January and February 2002, a series of meetings were scheduled for Belgrade and Brussells, but as Javier Solana (defense chief for the E.U.) explained quite bluntly, the continued dispute over separation was retarding rather than hastening entry into the European Union. The Montenegrin government seemed pulled in two directions: Eager for acceptance into the European Union but afraid to go back on their promise to gain Montenegrin independence, they continued to speak of the existing federation as impractical and outmoded with a bad currency and too many restrictions on business and trade, but they did not rule out a union of equal and sovereign states. In the context this might mean anything, from Switzerland to something like the North American Free Trade Agreement. Plagued by scandals, bullied by the European Union, Djukanović was watching his domestic support melt away and dreading the approach of the tourist season that might be adversely affected by international reports on continued conflict over separation.[15]

Facing the possibility of being deserted by his NATO supporters, Djukanović still did not mend fences with Belgrade, despite attempts by President Koštunica to improve relations. Djukanović's refusal to mend fences may not have been his own decision, since the U.S. State Department had always favored Zoran Djindjić—an old Milošević's crony—to push aside Koštunica, who was widely regarded as too honest for his own (or rather the U.S.'s) good. In casting about for allies and economic partners, Djukanović's government really had only one option: Croatia, the perennial guiding star of Montenegrin separatism, and Montenegrin representatives were soon going to Zagreb to make Štedimlija's dream a reality.

A clever man should have been able to read the handwriting on the wall. A forced and illegitimate secession would do little to integrate Montenegro into the economic life of Europe, and in making himself dictator, Djukanović would be following in the footsteps of his political mentor in Belgrade, now languishing in the Hague. Milošević had been given every chance to get out, but egged on by his militant wife, he had held on to the bitter end. For Djukanović, there was a way out: He might cut a deal with Belgrade (and perhaps with friendly Western governments) that he would abide by the Montenegrin constitution and the principles of fairness that would doom the referendum. In return, the president and his colleagues could hope to avoid international investigations that could prove dangerous as well as embarrassing.

Djukanović faced another dilemma, one that is well known to the separatist Parti Québecois in Canada. The PQ is able to win provincial elections—sometimes quite handsomely—and to form one government after another in Quebec, but it has nevertheless suffered defeats in referenda on full independence from Canada. A defeat would spell the end of Djukanović's political career, just as Jacques Parizeau had to go after the PQ narrowly lost the 1995 referendum. On the other hand, if Djukanović were to prevaricate and try to dodge the issue, the Liberals would probably desert him, thus forcing a new election.

Milo Djukanović, although he was still publicly pretending that Yugoslavia no longer really existed, may have secretly wished to postpone the referendum on Montenegro's sovereignty. He was aware (if only from opinion polls) that many of the voters who had supported him politically in the past would not necessarily vote for Montenegro's complete separation from Serbia, and a tactic of muddling through for several years, without resolving the question, might have seemed the least unsatisfactory "solution," and not only for him personally. A deteriorating and conflict-ridden federal union would not only keep the Yugoslav government weak but would favor Serbian president Zoran Djindjić, (whose rise to power was supported openly by the U.S. government) at the expence of his rival Vojislav Koštunica, the federal president. From this perspective, Western pressures on Djukanović to back down may have been merely a diplomatic ploy that allowed the Montenegrin President to defuse the crisis without losing face with his own supporters.

Under Western pressure, President Djukanović agreed to content himself with incomplete independence. The agreement on a newconstitutional system for a common state of Serbia and Montenegro brokered by the European Union on March 14, 2002, put Montenegrin separatists' ambitions on hold for three years. Common institutions will include a single-chamber parliament, a president, a "council of ministers" or government, and a court. The council of ministers has five departments—external relations, defense, international economic relations, domestic economic relations, and the protection of human and minority rights. A supreme defense council consisting of three members—the presidents of the common state and of the two republics—make decisions on the basis of consensus. Recruits serve on the territory of their home republic with the opportunity to serve in the other member republic at their request. A special system of voting in parliament—a policy, in effect, of "reverse discrimination"—allows Montenegro parity with Serbia, which has a population of ten million to Montenegro's 650,000.

Federal President Koštunica declared, "At a time when Europe is integrating and when the Balkans are threatened with disintegration, Serbia and Montenegro have moved along the road of integration and thereby are investing into the stability not only of the Balkans but also in stability and peace in Europe as well." The EU's Solana was equally upbeat: "We have together taken an important step forward for the stability of the region and for the stability of Europe." Solana also suggested the new arrangement marks "the beginning of a new chapter" that he says will lead Serbs and Montenegrins to eventual membership in the European Union.

Ironically, in March 1999 when Javier Solana was secretary general of NATO he signed the papers authorizing the airstrikes that effectively tore one part of Yugoslavia, Kosovo, from Serbia. The breathtaking cynicism of his subsequent role as the common state's savior is considered impolite to emphasize in Belgrade, however. Among the advocates of union with Serbia in Montenegro there are those who suspect that Solana had actually saved Djukanović's political skin by giving him an excuse not to go ahead with the referendum that many believe he was going to lose. Furthermore, they say, the new arrangement is tantamount to confederacy, with each republic creating its own currency (dinar in Serbia, euro in Montenegro) and its own banking and customs system.

Independent Church?

The most bizarre strategy of Montenegrin separatists was their pretense that they had founded an independent Montenegrin Church. Their goal was clear enough. Virtually every independent nation of Orthodox believers had its own autocephalous church: Greeks, Russians, Bulgarians, Serbs. Even countries of mixed Catholic and Orthodox population, such as Ukraine and Rumania, had their own churches, so why not Montenegro? "If wishes were horses, beggars would ride," goes an old English nursery rhyme, and the separatists faced two insurmountable obstacles.

The first obstacle is the unavoidable fact that, throughout the history of Montenegro, there has never been an autocephalous church. In the centuries before St. Sava established the Serbian patriarchate, Montenegrin Christians were subordinate to either Rome or Constantinople. Later, Catholics along the littoral were generally under the jurisdiction of the Catholic archbishopric of Bar, while the Orthodox metropolitanate was part of the Serbian patriarchate. As we have seen, the dissolution of the patriarchate (on two different occasions) forced Montenegrin archbishops to receive consecration at the hands of either the Serbian metropolitan within the Hapsburg Empire or from the Russian Church.

The second obstacle was not historical but current reality. The metropolitinate of Mon-

Metropolitan Amfilohije Radović

tenegro, and its able Metropolitan, Amfilohije Radović (along with his suffragan bishop and all his priests) were utterly and completely loyal to the Serbian patriarchate. In the event of Montenegrin independence, it would be up to the Metropolitan Amfilohije to decide whether or not to petition the Serbian patriarch and the ecumenical patriarch in Constantinople to raise the metropolitantate to the status of an autocephalous church.

The separatists pointed to the example of the Macedonian Church, which declared itself independent of the Serbian Church. This act, though uncanonical, was made by the legitimate bishops of Macedonia. Such a move was inconceivable in Montenegro.

The separatists were daunted neither by truth nor reality and arranged for one Mr. Miraš Dedeić to proclaim himself "metropolitan" of an independent Montenegrin Church. As a student, Dedeić had been viewed with suspicion as a probable agent planted into the Orthodox Church, and his divorce from his wife only confirmed doubts about his commitments. His unclerical behavior led to his being defrocked, then excommunicated, and ultimately anathematized—by the Ecumenical Patriarch in Constantinople (under whose jurisdiction he had served). His sect had no canonically recognized clergy, and most of the "faithful" consist of former Communist Party hacks and separatists who have never taken part in Church life. Calling himself "Bishop Mihailo," Dedeić opened up an office in Cetinje and began recruiting followers among ex-communists, atheists, and Albanians, who began attacking priests and attempting to occupy churches.

Although Djukanović, in his early days, had seen the wisdom of working with, rather than against, the metropolitinate, Montenegrin authorities refused to protect the Orthodox Church from the outrages committed by Dedeić's goons. On one occasion, Fr. Radomir Nikčević was driven to barricade himself in Vlaška Church in Cetinje. Dedeić, who claimed possession of all Orthodox churches in Montenegro, has not denied either the attempted church seizures or police support, though he does insist (against many eyewitness accounts) that no violence was committed.

The Orthodox Church worldwide has naturally refused to give any countenance to Dedeić's shenanigans. Metropolitan Meliton Karas, chief secretary for the ecumenical patriarchate's Holy and Sacred Synod, stated publicly that Dedeić was "no longer a member of the clergy of the Orthodox Church," that he was "non-canonically elevated to bishop," and that he had "proclaimed himself leader of the non-existent church of Montenegro." If this were not sufficient, the Ecumenical Patriarch Bartholomew wrote President Djukanović a grave letter (in April 2000) warning him against supporting "the person falsely representing himself as one of the bishops of the Orthodox church," a man who had been "defrocked and disentitled as after priest"

Support for the true metropolitanate is not limited to the Orthodox hierarchy. There is no place on earth where the Orthodox Church has been more active and more successful than in Montenegro. The widespread revival of religious faith (common in postcommunist societies) can be measured by the booming number of clerical ordinations and by the tremendous construction and reconstruction projects undertaken by the Church. The speaker of the Montenegrin parliament, Svetozar Marović, expressed outrage (on December 18, 2001) over the attack on Fr. Radomir and declared that "Montenegrin government bodies should do everything possible to secure respect for law and order." Marović, who belonged to the pragmatic wing of the current government in Montenegro, was aware of the need to attract foreign capital; perhaps he knew that. Until Montenegro,developed a respect for private property and a respect for contract law, it would never attract Western investment. If the violations of the property rights against the Orthodox Church became more broadly known in the West the hope of Western investment will evaporate.

Montenegrin Prospects

If Milo Djukanović was serious about a rapprochement with the West, his continued refusal to protect the rights of the Orthodox Church might prove to be a stumbling block. When followers of Miraš Dedeić, claiming to be supported by the Montenegrin Ministry of Religion, seized two churches on an island on Lake Skutari (Skadar), the Djukanović government adopted a "neutral" policy, refusingaccess to either the hooligans or the rightful owners, that is, the Orthodox Church.[17] In January 2002, the Metropolitan, in the course of a speech calling for peace and brotherhood, made a characteristic reference to a piece of Montenegrin folklore about an evil emperor of Duklja (*i.e.*, the Roman Emperor Diocletian), who had stirred up animosities. The king had been nailed to a bridge, he said, and that was the fate reserved for those who stirred up hatred. The Podgorica daily *Vijesti* reported on the speech, maliciously characterizing it as a call for a lynching.

The line was drawn in the sand. *Vijesti* was a supporter of Djukanović as well as an ally of George Soros—the international "philanthropist" who has more than once expressed his hostility to Christianity. The Metropolitan not only defended his speech, describing it as "a call on Montenegrins to nail to Vezirov Bridge the hatred of God, fratricide, disunity and conflict," but went on to sue the newspaper for libel.[18]

In suing a newspaper funded by Mr. Soros, Metropolitan Amfilohije undoubtedly understood that there was more at issue than libel. On the one side stood an authentic defender of Montenegro's authentic traditions, which are Christian, Orthodox, Serbian, and Montenegrin; arrayed against him—and the true and historic Montenegro—are all the forces of transnational capital and the international order. The odds would seem impossible, almost as impossible as the odds facing Christians in the third century, when they were being hounded to death by one of the greatest rulers of the first international order, the Illyrian-born Emperor Diocletian, still known in Montenegro as the evil Car Dukljanin.

Since 1389, Serbs have been saying that Prince Lazar had vowed his people to be a heavenly people. Perhaps never since Lazar's time have any Serbs been given so clear a choice, and never in modern times has any people faced the choice offered to Montenegrins: Whether to be true to their nation and their faith or to sacrifice their inheritance for a mess of pottage.

Notes

For the evolution of the Yugoslav constitution, Lampe is the best source in English. Other aspects of Tito's regime are covered by Beloff, Shoup, and Dedijer *et al.* For the period since the 1980's, the sources are more ephemeral and harder to evaluate: newspaper articles and published 'interviews, as well as personal conversations and direct observation.

1. Predrag Vukić, "Partizanske egzekucije na Cetinju."

2. Bogoljub Kočović. *Žrtve Drugog svetskog rata u Jugoslaviji.*

3. Fleming, "The Federal Principle."

4. Lampe, pp. 285ff.

5. Lampe, p. 314.

6. For Brković's interview for the Croat daily *Vjesnik* in March 2000, see *www.monitor.hr/vjesnik/2000/05/02/*.

7. This account was given by Ćosić to a Western journalist, who told it in an interview for this book.

8. Gelbard's Senate testimony to the Senate Foreign Relations Committee was given on July 29, 1999.

9. *Christian Science Monitor*, May 21, 1998.

10. For Bulatović and Milošević, see Branko Vujić, Aimpress.org, January 10, 2001.

11. OSCE statement, April 23, 2001; British Helsinki Human Rights Organization, "Election 2000."

12. Nicholas Forster, Sead Husić, *Financial Times*, August 9, 2001.

13. Institute for War and Peace Reporting, August 24, 2001.

14. Interview with Koštunica, Voice of America, report by Tanjug, January 3, 2001.

15. See reports on this crucial period, from Medijaklub and AIM websites, a well as Mišo Vujović, Duga.

16. Frank Brown, Religious News Service/AP, 11/28/2000.

17. *Politika*, February 6, 2002.

18. Information Service of the Serbian Orthodox Church, January 29, 2002.

Select Bibliography

Since this is a book aimed at a popular, English-speaking readership, scholarly annotation is kept to a minimum and preference is given to credible works available in English.

Istorija naroda Jugoslavije, vol. I (Beograd 1953).

Istorija srpskog naroda, vols. I & II (Beograd, 1994).

Narodna enciklopedija, vol. IV, *s.v.* "Crna Gora" (Zagreb, 1929).

Srednjovekovni srpski spisi o Kosovu (Beograd 1993).

The Serbian Question in the Balkans, written and assembled by members of the Geography Faculty, University of Belgrade (Belgrade, 1995).

History of Serbian Culture, tr. R.A. Major (Edgevare, England, 1995).

Ljetopis popa Dukljanina, Latinski tekst sa hrvatskim prijevodom i "Hrvatska kronika" (Zagreb, 1950).

Avakumovich, Ivan. *Mihailovich According to German Sources* (London, 1969).

Banac, Ivo. *The National Question in Yugoslavia since 1945* (Cambridge, 1979).

Barker, Elisabeth. *British Policy in the Balkans During World War II* (Zagreb, 1978).

Bataković, Dušan. "Ujedinjenje Crne Gore i Srbije: Od snova predaka do košmara savremenika," a 1999 speech available on Projekat Rastko (*www.Rastko.org.yu*).

Beloff, Nora. *Tito's Flawed Legacy: Yugoslavia and the West since 1939* (Boulder, CO/London, 1985).

Boehm, Christopher. *Blood Revenge: The Enactment and Management of Conflict in Montenegro and Other Tribal Societies*, revised edition (University of Pennsylvania, 1987).

Bury, J.B. *History of the Later Roman Empire*, reprint (New York, 1958).

Ćapin, Djordje. "Relationship Toward Serbian Monuments in Konavle," lecture given in Bijeljina May 1995, tr. Dejan Djurović (*www.Rastko.org.yu*).

Čemović, Predrag. "Od Podgorice do Gradiške," *Glasnik društva "Njegoš,"* vol. VII (June 1961) pp. 45-88.

Ciano, Count Galeazzo. *The Ciano Diaries*, 1939-1943, ed. Hugh Gibson

(Garden City, NY, 1945).

Ćirković, Sima. "Rises and Falls in Serbian Statehood in the Middle Ages," in *A History of Serbian Culture*.

Clissold, Stephen. *A Short Story of Yugoslavia*. Cambridge University Press, 1986.

Deakin, F. W. D. *The Embattled Mountain*. London: Oxford University Press, 1971.

Dedijer, Vladimir, Ivan Božić, Sima Ćirković, and Milorad Ekmečić. *History of Yugoslavia* (New York, 1974).

Djilas, Milovan. *Land Without Justice*, tr. M.B. Petrovich (New York, 1954).

----. *Montenegro*, tr. Kenneth Johnstone (London, 1964).

----. *Njegoš—Poet, Prince, Bishop* (New York, 1966).

----. *Parts of a Lifetime*, ed. M. and D. Milenkovitch (New York, 1975).

----. *Wartime* (New York & London, 1977).

Dragnich, Alex N. *Serbs and Croats: The Struggle in Yugoslavia* (New York, 1992).

----. *The First Yugoslavia* (Stanford, CA, 1983).

Drljević, Sekula. *Balkanski sukobi*, 1905-1941 (Zagreb, 1944).

Dvornik, Francis. *The Slavs: Their Early History and Civilization* (Boston, 1952).

Errington, R.M. *A History of Macedonia*, tr. by Catherine Errington (New York, 1990).

Ferluga, Jadran. *L'Amministrazione bizantina in Dalmazia* (Venezia, 1978).

Fine, J.V.A. Jr. *The Early Medieval Balkans: A Critical Survey From the Sixth to the Late Twelfth Century* (Ann Arbor, MI, 1983).

----. *The Late Medieval Balkans: A Critical Survey from the Late Twelfth Century to the Ottoman Conquest* (Ann Arbor, 1982).

Fleming, Thomas J. *The Politics of Human Nature* (Brunswick, NJ, 1988).

----."A League of Our Own," *Chronicles: A Magazine of American Culture* (February, 1993).

----."America's Crack-up," *National Review* (July 28, 1997).

----. "The Federal Principle," *Telos* 100 (1994), pp. 17-36.

Ford, Kirk, Jr. *OSS and the Yugoslav Resistance 1943-1945*. (College Station, TX, 1992).

Gopčević, Spiridion. *Geschichte von Montenegro und Albanien* (Gotha, 1914).

Hoptner, Jakob. *Yugoslavia in Crises, 1934-1941*. New York and London, 1962.

Hehn, Paul. *The German Struggle Against Yugoslav Guerrillas in World War II, 1941-1945* (New York, 1979).

Jelavich, Barbara. *History of the Balkans*, vol. 1, Eighteenth and Nineteenth Centuries (Cambridge, 1983).

----. *History of the Balkans*, vol. 2, Twentieth Century (Cambridge, 1983).

Kočović, Bogoljub. *Žrtve Drugog svetskog rata u Jugoslaviji* (Harrow, 1985).

Lampe, John. *Yugoslavia as History: Twice There Was a Country*, 2nd ed. (Cambridge, 2000).

Lees, Michael. *The Rape of Serbia* (San Diego, 1990).

Loi, Salvatore. *Jugoslavia 1941* (Torino, 1953).

Marković, C. and R. Vujičić. *The Cultural Monuments of Montenegro/Spomenici kulture Crne Gore* (Novi Sad, 1997).

Martin, David. *Patriot or Traitor* (Stanford, CA, 1978).

McNeill, W.H. *Venice: the Hinge of Europe, 1081-1797* (Chicago, 1974).

Marriot, Sir John A.R. *The Eastern Question: An Historical Study in European Diplomacy*, 4th edition (Oxford, 1940).

Matavulj, Simo. *Boka i Bokelji* (Novi Sad, 1893).

Medaković, B.M.G. *Crnogorskim uskocima* (Beograd, 1895).

----. *Petar Petrović II Njegoš* (Novi Sad, 1882).

Mihailovic, Dragoslav. *Goli Otok* (Belgrade, 1990).

Mijović, Pavle. *Od Dokleje do Podgorice* (Cetinje, 1998).

Minić, Fr. Mihailo. *Rasute kosti, 1941-1945* (Detroit, 1965)

Nenadović, Ljubomir. *Pisma iz Italije* (Zagreb, 1950).

Njegoš, Petar II Petrović. *Sabrana djela*, 7 vols. (Podgorica, 2001).

Njegoš, Petar II Petrović. *The Mountain Wreath*, tr. V.D. Mihailovich (Belgrade, 1997).

Norwich, John Julius. *A History of Venice* (New York, 1982).

Orbini, Mauro. *Il regno degli Slavi* (Pesaro, 1601).

Ostrogorsky, George. *History of the Byzantine State* (Rutgers University, 1969).

Pavićević, Branko. *Crna Gora u ratu 1862*, ed. With French resume by Jorjo Tadić (Beograd, 1963).

Pavlovich, Paul. *The Serbians: The Story of a People* (Toronto, 1983).

Pešić, Desanka. *Jugoslovenski komunisti i nacionalno pitanje*, (Belgrade 1983).

Petrović, Kralj Nikola. *Memoari*, (Cetinje, 1988).

Petrovich, M.B. *A History of Modern Serbia*, 2 vols. (New York, 1976).

Phrantzes, Georgios. *The Fall of the Byzantine Empire*, tr. Marios Philippides (Amherst, MA, 1980).

Podesta, Giuseppe. *Sorella Prigionia* (Oliginate, 1990).

Popović, Djordje. *Istorija Crne Gore* (Beograd, 1896).

Radan, Peter and Aleksandar Pavković. *The Serbs and Their Leaders in the Twentieth Century* (Aldershot, 1997).

Roberts, Walter R. *Tito, Mihailovich, and the Allies 1941-1945* (New Brunswick, NJ, 1969).

Redžić, Vučeta. *"Pasje groblje" u Kolašinu* (Beograd 1999).

Shoup, Paul. *Communism and the Yugoslav National Question* (New York, 1968).

Seton-Watson, Robert. *The Southern Slav Question and the Habsburg Monarchy* (London, 1911).

Soulis, George C. *The Serbs and Byzantium During the Reign of Tsar Stephen Dusan* (Washington, D.C., 1984).

Spasojević, Jovo ("Montenegrinus"). *Ujedinjene Crne Gore sa Srbijom* (Geneva, 1917)

Stamatović, Aleksandar. *Kratka istorija Mitropolije Crnogorsko-primorske* (Cetinje, 1999).

Stephenson, Francis S. *A History of Montenegro* (London, 1912).

Südland L.v. [Ivo Pilar] *Die südslawische Frage und der Weltkrieg: Übersichtliche Darstellung des Gesamt-Problems* (Wien, 1918).

Sumner, B. H. *Peter the Great and the Ottoman Empire* (Oxford, 1949).

Temperley, Harold W.V. *History of Serbia* (London, 1917).

Terzić, Slavenko. "Ideological Roots of Montenegrin Nation and Montenegrin Separatism," tr. Stefan Branisavljević (*www.Njegos.org*, ed. Aleksandar Raković).

Terzić, Velimir. *Jugoslavija u aprilskom ratu*, 1941 (Titograd, 1963).

Tolstoy, Nikolai. *The Minister and the Massacres* (London, 1986).

Toynbee, Arnold. *Constantine Porphyrogenitus and his World* (Oxford, 1973).

Trifković, Srdja. "Prince Pavle Karadjordević" in Radan and Pavković, pp. 158-202.

----. *Ustaša: Croatian Separatism and European Politics, 1929-1945* (London, 1998)

Vasiliev, A. *A History of the Byzantine Empire*, 2 vols. (Madison, WI, 1952).

Velimirovich, Bishop Nikolai and Archimandrite Justin Popovich, *The Mystery and the Meaning of the Battle of Kosovo*, tr. Rt. Rev. Todor Mikla and Rev. Stevan Scott (Skokie, IL, 1989).

Vukić, Predrag. "Partizanske egzekucije na Cetinju u novembru 1944," *Glasnik društva "Njegoš,"* No. 78 (May 1998).

Walbank, F.W. *A Historical Commentary on Polybius*, 3 vols. (Berkeley, 1957-79).

West, Richard. *Tito, and the Rise and Fall of Yugoslavia* (New York, 1994).

Wilkes. J.J. *Dalmatia* (Cambridge, MA, 1969).